CENTRE FOR EDUCATIONAL RESEARCH AND INNOVATION

Special Needs Education

Statistics and Indicators

OECD

ORGANISATION FOR ECONOMIC CO-OPERATION AND DEVELOPMENT

ORGANISATION FOR ECONOMIC CO-OPERATION AND DEVELOPMENT

Pursuant to Article 1 of the Convention signed in Paris on 14th December 1960, and which came into force on 30th September 1961, the Organisation for Economic Co-operation and Development (OECD) shall promote policies designed:

- to achieve the highest sustainable economic growth and employment and a rising standard of living in Member countries, while maintaining financial stability, and thus to contribute to the development of the world economy;
- to contribute to sound economic expansion in Member as well as non-member countries in the process of economic development; and
- to contribute to the expansion of world trade on a multilateral, non-discriminatory basis in accordance with international obligations.

The original Member countries of the OECD are Austria, Belgium, Canada, Denmark, France, Germany, Greece, Iceland, Ireland, Italy, Luxembourg, the Netherlands, Norway, Portugal, Spain, Sweden, Switzerland, Turkey, the United Kingdom and the United States. The following countries became Members subsequently through accession at the dates indicated hereafter: Japan (28th April 1964), Finland (28th January 1969), Australia (7th June 1971), New Zealand (29th May 1973), Mexico (18th May 1994), the Czech Republic (21st December 1995), Hungary (7th May 1996), Poland (22nd November 1996) and Korea (12th December 1996). The Commission of the European Communities takes part in the work of the OECD (Article 13 of the OECD Convention).

The Centre for Educational Research and Innovation was created in June 1968 by the Council of the Organisation for Economic Co-operation and Development and all Member countries of the OECD are participants.

The main objectives of the Centre are as follows:

- *analyse and develop research, innovation and key indicators in current and emerging education and learning issues, and their links to other sectors of policy;*
- *explore forward-looking coherent approaches to education and learning in the context of national and international cultural, social and economic change; and*
- *facilitate practical co-operation among Member countries and, where relevant, with non-member countries, in order to seek solutions and exchange views of educational problems of common interest.*

The Centre functions within the Organisation for Economic Co-operation and Development in accordance with the decisions of the Council of the Organisation, under the authority of the Secretary-General. It is supervised by a Governing Board composed of one national expert in its field of competence from each of the countries participating in its programme of work.

Publié en français sous le titre :
BESOINS ÉDUCATIFS PARTICULIERS
Statistiques et indicateurs

FOREWORD

In 1995 the Centre for Educational Research and Innovation (CERI) published the first set of data making comparisons in the field of special needs education. This work strengthened the view that a different comparative framework would need to be developed if reliable and valid comparisons were to be made. In 1996 the first discussions began with countries on developing a resource based definition. This helps to overcome different national interpretations of concepts such as special educational needs which cover very different populations of students who are experiencing difficulties in accessing the curriculum.

At the same time the UNESCO standards for classifying education systems (ISCED) was in the process of being revised and the definition of special needs education was updated and reformulated to reflect policy developments. In doing so, a much wider range of students, in all types of schools, were brought into the frame. In addition, the idea that extra resourcing may be needed to assist schools to help students access the curriculum more effectively was included in the new description.

It became clear early on that for policy relevant comparisons to emerge, a resource based approach would require that the students included under this definition would need to be sub-divided into some form of straightforward classification scheme. Countries agreed on a tri-partite system in which students are divided into three cross-national categories, A, B and C. Briefly, they cover:

- students whose disabilities have clear biological causes (Category A);
- students who are experiencing learning difficulties for no particular reason (Category B); and
- students who have difficulties arising from disadvantages (Category C).

The data provided in this book are based on the application of this model in practice.

The book presents a complete account of the development of the work, and provides qualitative data to contextualise the quantitative information. It provides breakdowns by national category systems as well as comparisons using the cross-national framework described.

The work was partially supported by additional contributions from the US Department of Education, Office of Special Education and Rehabilitative Services (OSERS) and by DGXXII of the European Union.

The book was prepared by the chief consultant to the project Professor Colin Robson, and by Professor Peter Evans and Ms. Marcella Deluca of the OECD/CERI secretariat, in close collaboration with the countries involved. The authors would like to thank Mr Michael Bruneforth (OECD/SID) for his valuable technical advice and Mrs Maree Galland (OECD/CERI) for her administrative support. This book is published under the responsibility of the Secretary-General of the OECD.

TABLE OF CONTENTS

Chapter 1

INTRODUCTION

Background

Interest in the performance of national education systems has never been as strong as it is at present. All OECD Member countries are concerned with the standards attained by students and the type of learning that all our children and young people are engaged in, as educational reforms are planned and put in place as part of a strategy for moving our countries into the knowledge economy.

Students with disabilities, learning difficulties and disadvantages, who will be referred to in this monograph by the generic term "students with special educational needs" are no exception, and reform programmes are being developed to assist these students to improve their skills and to be included more fully into society and work. The demographic trends are such that in the coming years, as a result of the increasing numbers of retired citizens and the decreasing birth rate, all available skills will be needed to maintain our economies.

The gathering of statistics about and the development of indicators of education systems are viewed as indispensable to this endeavour, and the effort has been spearheaded by the OECD in collaboration with UNESCO and the European Union. However, it has been noticeable that the field of special educational needs has not been covered in any adequate way with the result that relevant information is scarce.

In 1995, the OECD published the first comprehensive set of data intended to provide a comparative review of provision for students with disabilities and disadvantages in OECD countries. Although the work showed that the definitions used were so different among countries that comparisons were almost impossible to make, sufficiently large differences existed between countries to indicate the occurrence of substantial variations in provision.

The present monograph continues this work and describes the beginning of a process which is intended to improve the data quality of the database leading to better international comparability and policy decision-making in the field of education pertaining to disabled and disadvantaged students. It is a first attempt to provide an extensive set of comparable statistics across OECD Member countries, covering such a wide range of learning difficulties.

More recently, and providing additional motivation for a new initiative in this area, the instrument used for defining the nature of education statistics to be gathered internationally, the International Standard Classification of Education (ISCED), has been revised. In the original version of the classification, special education was defined as the education provided in special schools; a definition wholly out of keeping with both theory and practice in many countries, and which in itself limits interest in obtaining data in this area.

The new version of ISCED (ISCED-97) has attempted to put this right and provides the following definition of special education:

Special needs education: educational intervention and support designed to address *special educational needs*. The term "special needs education" has come into use as a replacement for the term "special education".

OECD 2000

The older term was mainly understood to refer to the education of children with disabilities that takes place in special schools or institutions distinct from, and outside of, the institutions of the regular school and university system. In many countries today a large proportion of disabled children are in fact educated in institutions of the regular system. Moreover, the concept of "children with special educational needs" extends beyond those who may be included in handicapped categories to cover those who are failing in school for a wide variety of other reasons that are known to be likely to impede a child's optimal progress. Whether or not this more broadly defined group of children are in need of additional support depends on the extent to which schools need to adapt their curriculum, teaching and organisation and/or to provide additional human or material resources so as to stimulate efficient and effective learning for these pupils (UNESCO, 1997).

It is clear that this definition substantially changes and updates the definition of special education especially in terms of resources made available, and it carries with it a requirement for a rather different operationalisation for the purposes of gathering statistics.

As noted above, earlier work had identified the difficulty in comparing data in special needs education among countries. Two outstanding problems were identified. First, the term "special needs education" means different things in different countries. In some it covers only children with traditional disabilities, while in others it includes a much wider range of students covering, for instance, disability, learning difficulty and disadvantage. Second, because of the wide variations in the definitions of disability and learning difficulty which are in use it remains unclear whether differences between quantitative estimates for any particular category from different countries are comparable. Furthermore, there has been in special educational circles particular concern about the lack of educational utility of descriptive categories which are derived from medical classifications. Disability categories are viewed as having only partial implications for educational provision or for the development of teaching programmes, which inevitably have to take the whole child into account. Therefore, categories based on medical descriptions are at best only of limited value to education policy-makers, which is the main purpose of data gathered within the ISCED framework at the OECD.

The points raised above argue, then, for a new approach and following proposals from the OECD Secretariat and discussions with Member countries it was decided to tackle the problem in the following way. In order to overcome the different definitions of special needs education that operate among countries, it was necessary to provide a means to identify and include all students for whom extra provision is made in order to help them make progress through the school curriculum.

It was decided to identify this envelope of students through a supply side approach based on resources made available. This has the advantage of being educationally-based and at the same time fits with the intent of the ISCED-97 definition.

Thus, the definition of special needs education agreed is that "those with special educational needs are defined by the additional public and/or private resources provided to support their education". The use of this definition in a consistent manner calls for agreement about the term ADDITIONAL and an appreciation of the various kinds of possible RESOURCES PROVIDED which should be considered.

Thus "Additional resources" are those made available over and above the resources generally available to students[1] where no consideration is given to needs of students likely to have particular difficulties in accessing the regular curriculum.

Resources can be of many different kinds:

- *Personnel resources*. These include a more favourable teacher/student ratio than in a regular classroom where no allowance is being made for students with special needs; additional teachers, assistants or any

---

1. The term "student" is used throughout the text. It is to be regarded as synonymous with "pupil" or "(school) child".

other personnel (for some or all of the time); training programmes for teachers and others which equip them for work in special needs education.

- *Material resources*. These include aids or supports of various types (*e.g.* hearing aid); modifications or adaptations to classroom; specialised teaching materials.

- *Financial resources*. These include funding formulae which are more favourable to those with special needs (including classes where it is known or assumed that there are students with special needs); systems where money is set aside for special educational needs within the regular budget allocation; payments made in support of special needs education; and the costs of personnel and material resources.

The key question is whether these resources are made available to support students education and are provided when they have particular difficulties in accessing the regular curriculum.

One result of the resources approach is that it brings together students with learning difficulties with very different causes, and it was recognised that a group formed in this way would itself need to be further sub-divided. To achieve this, a tri-partite categorisation system was devised based on perceived causes of educational failure. Countries are asked to re-classify the data into this framework based on the classification and data collection arrangements used in their own national system following the operational definitions provided.

Operational definitions of cross-national categories

The three categories which were agreed are called A, B and C and are defined as follows.

Category A: refers to educational needs of students where there is substantial normative agreement – such as blind and partially sighted, deaf and partially hearing, severe and profound mental handicap, multiple handicaps. These conditions affect students from all social classes and occupations. Typically, adequate measuring instruments and agreed criteria are available. In medical terms, they are considered as being organic disorders attributable to organic pathologies (*e.g.* in relation to sensory, motor or neurological defects).

Category B: refers to educational needs of students who have difficulties in learning which do not appear to be directly or primarily attributable to factors which would lead to categorisation as "A" or "C".

Category C: refers to educational needs of students which are considered to arise primarily from socio-economic, cultural and/or linguistic factors. There is some form of disadvantaged or atypical background for which education seeks to compensate.

In the following chapters, these ideas and descriptions are elaborated upon and data gathered within this new framework are presented. The next chapter provides an outline of the methodology used to develop the data collection instrument, which is supplied at the end of the text.

Notes

The work reported here has benefited from close collaboration between the OECD/CERI secretariat and country representatives. The data presented are therefore as accurate as possible.

In the report, comparisons are limited to primary and lower secondary education. This decision was made in the interest of data quality and availability. Outside of these educational periods, relevant data are much more difficult to obtain.

Symbols for missing data

Four symbols are employed in the tables and graphs to denote missing data:

a   Data not applicable because the category does not apply.

m   Data missing.

n   Magnitude is either negligible or nil.

x   Data included in another category/column of the table.

Codes for OECD Member countries

Australia	AUS	Korea	KOR
Austria	AUT	Luxembourg	LUX
Belgium	BEL	Mexico	MEX
Canada	CAN	Netherlands	NLD
Czech Republic	CZE	New Zealand	NZL
Denmark	DNK	Norway	NOR
Finland	FIN	Poland	POL
France	FRA	Portugal	PRT
Germany	DEU	Spain	ESP
Greece	GRC	Sweden	SWE
Hungary	HUN	Switzerland	CHE
Iceland	ISL	Turkey	TUR
Ireland	IRL	United Kingdom	UKM
Italy	ITA	United States	USA
Japan	JPN		

OECD 2000

Chapter 2

DEVELOPMENT OF THE DATA COLLECTION INSTRUMENT

Background

The data collection instrument needed to achieve the aims discussed in the previous chapter was developed in the autumn of 1996 and through 1997. Initial proposals were discussed at meetings of a small steering group consisting of OECD, UNESCO, EUROSTAT (the statistical arm of the European Community) and the Directorate General of Education, Training and Youth of the European Commission (DGXXII). Broad agreement was reached on the approach to be taken. In particular it was agreed that, in the first instance, it would be highly desirable for the instrument used in this study to follow the general approach, terminology and conventions of the already existing UOE (UNESCO/OECD/EUROSTAT) data collection exercise. A very substantial amount of information about the nature and working of national educational systems has been collected yearly under the joint auspices of these three organisations.

In the UOE data collection exercise, data relating to special educational needs were restricted to the number of students in special schools which, as discussed in the previous chapter, gives only a partial and, in many countries, misleading and inappropriate picture of the extent of provision for students with special needs. It was agreed that by seeking to link this study conceptually to the wider UOE exercise there would be the advantage that in many countries persons responsible for collecting statistical information nationally might be involved with completing entries for this study on special needs, and hence find the task more manageable. It was also seen as a long term aim that, if this initial study demonstrated the feasibility of the approach taken, then this form of data collection about special educational needs would be incorporated into the general data collection exercise.

Meeting of national representatives

The approach agreed by the steering group formed the basis of proposals made to a meeting of country representatives and experts in October 1996. This meeting was mainly composed of representatives of OECD Member countries but there was also representation from UNESCO.

The meeting achieved its objectives of agreeing the conceptual framework of the study, the initial data to be gathered, and the scope and country involvement of a set of pilot studies. These latter studies were to examine and discuss the issues raised by this type of data collection. In particular they were seen as a means of trying to establish the types of data which were likely to be readily available because they are already collected nationally, together with those types of data which while not currently collected nationally would both be of interest for the country concerned, and be collectable without major additional resource implications.

Representatives from each of the countries present at the meeting gave a presentation which highlighted their national educational system as it relates to special needs, and the relevant statistical information which was collected. A striking feature of these presentations was that in virtually all cases the system in relation to special educational needs provision was reported to be in a state of transition. A very common feature was a move toward inclusiveness (*i.e.* away from a separate system for students and pupils with special educational needs in schools and units which are physically and administratively separated, and towards one where these students receive their education in regular schools and classrooms). This was seen as, in part, linked to the large number of nations who seek to fulfil the United Nations standard rules on persons with special needs and more generally with drives toward equity in provision.

Almost equally commonly mentioned was a move toward decentralising educational systems so that decisions and responsibilities (*e.g.* in relation to resource allocations) were taken at lower levels (*e.g.* at municipality rather than at state or regional level). While this latter feature is not specific to special needs provision it does appear to raise particular issues in this field perhaps because of its complex nature. It also is likely to make the collection of statistical information at national level substantially more difficult.

The attempt of the study to use a resource allocation definition of special educational needs was seen as problematic both in practical data collection terms (*e.g.* it may be difficult to specify how many pupils have extra resources of a particular kind but it may be feasible to specify the totality of resources made available for a particular need) and politically (*e.g.* in influencing the number of children with a right to such resources) by several representatives, but was strongly supported by others as a way of avoiding categorical definitions. Some means of assessing the quality of provision was advocated.

The importance of a statutory framework for special needs provision which clearly specified parents' and pupils' rights was stressed by several representatives.

Many representatives emphasised the timeliness of the study in that forms of integrated provision for pupils with special needs are not captured within the current UOE data collection exercise and the decentralisation of resource provision raises complexities in the current approach. Such points were made strongly by these representatives as strengthening their support for the study, which was seen as addressing issues of direct relevance to their own systems as well as its primary function of facilitating meaningful international comparisons between systems.

There was a clear consensus of support for the purposes of the study and for the conceptual framework as explained in the study outline and elaborated in the discussion document arising from the steering group meeting. The following issues were seen as important.

Linkage to UOE data collection exercise

The central concern of the study is the development of a data collection instrument, with the end product specified as a joint UNESCO/OECD/EUROSTAT recommendation to data providers to include the data collection instrument in the UOE data collection. It was seen as crucial that this central concern was kept firmly in mind throughout the study.

It was recognised that the revision of ISCED discussed in the previous chapter was still at a relatively fluid state and that the conceptualisation of special education in the revised ISCED was seen as potentially leading to problems. It was understood however that such a conceptualisation is open to reformulation. Several representatives stressed that great attention will have to be paid to the operationalisation of ISCED levels in relation to special educational needs provision in the revised version of ISCED.

The omission of the special educational needs dimension from the current UOE instrument, apart from numbers of students in segregated special schools, was a clearly perceived lack and is increasingly commented by Member countries. Many legislative frameworks now relate to persons with special needs and disabilities, and more generally concerns for equity of treatment call for information which can be used to monitor progress in these fields.

Operational definition of special educational needs

At that stage, special educational needs were defined by the additional public and/or private resources committed to them to support their education. [Note that this definition is not identical to that eventually adopted for the data collection exercise. Where the reference here is to resources committed, the final version (see Questionnaire at the end of the text) refers to resources provided ; see page 16 for an explanation of this change].

The proposed definition was an operationalised version of that in the version of the then current revision of the ISCED manual (the additional intervention and support needed by children and youth with disabilities and other recognised learning difficulties). This type of definition attempts to encompass a wide range of needs which are differentially labelled and categorised in national systems and where the provision is in different facilities including regular schools and regular classrooms.

After lengthy discussion which revealed many of the complexities linked to this kind of resource-allocation based definition, it was agreed that the working definition should be adopted for the study but that it should continue to be refined as the study progresses.

Categorisation of special educational needs

This topic also generated much discussion, in part because there is a growing movement in national systems which are implementing integrated provision in regular school settings for those with special educational needs in order to avoid such categorisation. However many systems do continue to employ various forms of categorisation which could provide useful data. It will also help link this study to the previously used categories based on disability. A consensus was achieved in favour of employing a simple categorisation system in the pilot work, while recognising that there will be practical difficulties for national systems which do not categorise.

It was agreed at the meeting that a tri-partite scheme should be adopted covering *a*) the "2%" (or students with the most clear impairments), *b*) learning disabled, and *c*) disadvantaged/compensatory (NB: these are shorthand terms). It was accepted that major amplification and exemplification would be needed to clarify their meaning and assist in the provision of comparable information. It was also agreed that for post-compulsory education a fourth category, covering those who had not previously been identified, should be added and that respondents be asked to provide a single global figure relating to those falling within the operational definition in their country. They would also be invited to split this down into the subcategories which they used.

Educational indicators

The development of appropriate education indicators in the domain of special education was agreed as the second central thrust of the project. Possible approaches were explored and suggestions made. For example, in connection with indicating the extent to which a system treats all persons equitably, an approach might be to identify barriers in the system to such equality of treatment, whether at the simple level of physical access or in relation to flexibility of curriculum. It appeared that the goal should be the development of a small set of powerful indicators.

Initial data to be gathered

It was agreed that a prototype version of a data collection instrument to fulfil the purposes of the study, and cover the issues noted above, should be developed by the consultant in discussion with the secretariat.

This would be followed by study visits to eight countries to test the viability of the instrument and to gather pilot data. The visits were planned to start before the end of 1996 and to be completed in 1997. Countries likely to be faced with different issues and problems in completing the data collection instrument (and in particular in completing it in a manner which produced reliable and valid data, comparable across countries) should be chosen. It was envisaged that the data collection instrument would be developed over this set of visits in an iterative manner.

Scope and country involvement of the pilot visits

It was agreed that the countries should be selected by the secretariat, after the meeting, through discussion with representatives of the countries. Criteria for choice should include willingness to be involved, and the countries selected should reflect differing political organisational structures (*e.g.* Federal and non-Federal states), different educational structures (*e.g.* concerning extent of integration of disabled pupils), and regional variation (*e.g.* Europe, North America). While it would be desirable to include varied regional representation there appears to be such major variation within region that regionality in itself is not an appropriate variable. Representation from developing countries should also being sought.

Given the severely limited set of visits it was crucial that the choice of country participation be strongly influenced by the extent to which the host countries would be both prepared and able to devote resources to provide detailed feedback and support on the data collection exercise. There was a very encouraging response from national representatives at the October 1996 meeting, with several indicating their willingness to be involved with this pilot work.

These arrangements were then followed by a meeting of the steering group to discuss outcomes and to plan for a later meeting of country representatives which would also discuss outcomes and agree the time-frame for the gathering of a more extensive data set using the modified version of the instrument. Following collection and analysis of data and calculation of experimental indicators for publication at the end of the study there would be meetings to discuss outcomes and future developments.

Pilot visits

Eight countries, selected to reflect different political structures and educational organisation, were visited over the time-scale envisaged above. They comprised six OECD countries [Belgium (Flemish Community), Denmark, Hungary, the Netherlands, Switzerland and the United States] and two developing countries (Sri Lanka and Zambia). Short notes on the points and issues raised by the visits are presented below. As the opportunity was taken to develop and refine the proposed data collection instrument from the feedback obtained in successive visits, the notes are given here in the chronological order in which the visits took place.

Switzerland

This visit was in the nature of a pre-pilot in that the version of the data collection instrument discussed on the visit was in a very tentative draft form. The main intention was to establish those areas where data were likely to be available and the problems for national data collection posed by a strong regional (cantonal) system.

Meetings were organised with representatives of the Swiss Federal Statistical Office and with representatives with similar responsibilities in a number of cantons. A colloquium at the Institut für Sonderpadagogik (Institute for Special Education) on the special study attended by a range of interested parties involved in the Swiss educational system stimulated a wide spectrum of comments.

A visit to the canton of Fribourg and detailed discussions with those responsible for collecting their statistical information on students with special educational needs was very helpful in grounding the earlier discussions in the reality of their situation.

Subsequent written responses to questions raised by the data collection instrument from the statisticians at the Ministry of Education, collated by Dr. Hollenweger, of the Institut fur Sonderpadagogik, University of Zurich, were used in developing a revised version of the instrument to be used on later visits.

Denmark

Denmark is an example of a country with a strong commitment to inclusive education in the form of the school for all. It also has considerable decentralisation in its educational system which appears likely to make the collection of detailed national statistics more difficult. The same draft instrument was used as on the visit to Switzerland.

The visit involved discussions with representatives of the Ministry of Education including those with responsibilities for special educational needs, advisers responsible for the development of quality in the Danish basic school, participation in OECD work, and the statistical department.

A visit to a county (Roskilde), a municipality within that county and a school within the municipality; and discussions with persons at each of these levels in the system was extremely valuable in exploring their different perspectives particularly in relation to the likely availability of relevant statistical data.

Ministry representatives responsible for special educational needs expressed considerable interest in making international comparisons in this area in order to inform policies on equity and inclusion. They were also enthusiastic about developing indicators in this area. The Ministry publishes its own education indicators of which only one relates to special education ("Number and percentage of pupils receiving special education in Folkeskole: 12.6% in 1994/95"). The actual statistic is pupils who, in the course of the school year, have received special needs education for a shorter or longer period of time and covers pupils in ordinary schools and classes as well as those in special schools. It does not show how much of, or which type of, special needs education the children received and does not cover private schools.

The resources definition was generally viewed as acceptable. The fact that some of the resources for those with special needs come from Social and Health Departments was seen as likely to cause difficulties in obtaining the relevant information.

In general the database for pupils in the Folkeskole (*i.e.* for compulsory education) seems reasonable. Outside this age range the data are much more patchy. A different ministry deals with upper secondary and the strong advice given was to stick to compulsory education for the current exercise.

Within compulsory education data on the numbers in special schools and classes are satisfactory but numbers in regular classes would be an estimate. It was interesting to note that at county level there was the view that head count data on students with special needs in regular classes was available. However the representative from the municipality considered that decentralisation had now reached the stage where that information was solely accessible at school level.

What is referred to in Denmark as "organic handicaps" (which appears to correspond to cross-national Category A) has eight sub-categories under which data are collected at county level (see below on Legislative Framework). At national level, figures could be provided for compulsory school age in relation to "these categories" overall and in different settings separately. Figures on wider special needs in single categories could be provided for compulsory school age but might have to be an estimate.

The simple cross-national categorisation was viewed as broadly acceptable. Suggestions were made for slight reframing of the definitions so that they are not exclusively focused on the child but take note of what the school has to do to meet the identified needs. A proposal was also made for splitting the "learning disabilities" sub-category (subsequently referred to as cross-national Category B) in two to cover something like "normal with specific problems *e.g.* reading" and "low intellectual function".

The exercise of mapping national categories on to the cross-national categories was viewed very positively. There was a plea however for the possibility that a particular national category might be viewed as falling within two or more of the simple categories.

The visit concluded with a detailed résumé of the parts of the UOE data collection exercise where it would be feasible to obtain data relevant to special educational needs.

United States

The visit involved discussions with representatives of the US Department of Education, WESTAT (an organisation which holds contracts with the Department of Education for collection of educational statistical data in the special needs field), New York State and Maryland. This was to enable perspectives at both Federal and State level to be obtained. The discussions in relation to Maryland took place in Baltimore.

The visit was notable for the serious and detailed attention given to the special study and the revised draft version of the data collection instrument (which had been circulated prior to the visit), both in preparation for the visit and during the visit itself.

The federal and state representatives met during the visit were primarily involved with individuals with disabilities which represents a much more restricted concept of special needs than that embraced by the study. It was possible to get some information on wider needs (*e.g.* in relation to Title 1 covering disadvantaged/compensatory) but this was sketchy and largely hearsay.

This raises a general issue which has arisen in previous pilots: the resource-based definition, if taken seriously, may call on the involvement of many different national agencies over and above those directly responsible for special needs as defined in a particular country (*e.g.* Health; Social Services; Equal Rights; Civil Rights; Population Census; as well as other parts of education administration).

The cross-state standard format of statistical information available relevant to special needs is essentially limited to that required by federal law. The special needs field is advantageously placed in this respect in that there are several such laws (*e.g.* in relation to individuals with disabilities, provision of least restrictive environment, and delivery of equal rights) where federal funds are available to states and where the provision of such funds is conditional upon statistical returns being made. This simplifies the data collection task very considerably as essentially WESTAT holds much of these data and hence provides a single point of reference.

However it also sets severe limits on what is currently available, apparently excluding much special needs data on post-compulsory education, on educational personnel and on funding. It is likely that the data on persons with disabilities are substantially more detailed than other data sets. It appears that what states collect data-wise over-and-above that required for federal funding varies considerably from state to state, with some taking the view that they do not need to collect any such additional data. Nevertheless there did seem to be considerable goodwill from all representatives toward investigating ways in which additional data might be gathered for the purposes of the special study, possibly on a sample survey basis.

Several suggestions were made for educational indicators. These included:

a) Participation rates: how many special needs students are identified and served.

b) Placement data: extent to which they are educated with their peers.

c) School completion/drop-out.

d) Performance in tests/assessments.

e) Post-school outcome/employment.

f) Resource indicator: costs/expenditure per student.

g) Relative contributions of federal/state/local.

There were thought to be relatively good data for a & b above (although this is for individuals with disabilities only), substantially weaker for the rest.

There was some principled opposition to a resource-based definition and preference for continuing with a disability-driven definition. However the definition was agreed to be broadly acceptable as facilitating international comparability and a wide, inclusive, approach.

The definition in terms of resources committed was felt to be problematic in that resources might be committed (in the sense of it being accepted in some formal sense that they should be provided) but not actually provided. It may be that resources provided is better in operational terms.

Discussion confirmed the view from previous pilots that it was best to drop the category additional post-compulsory special needs in light of deficiencies in the post-compulsory database and the need to concentrate in the first instance on a central core of concerns.

Various other comments and criticisms were made of the labels and definitions of the simple cross-national categorisation of special needs, with some arguing for a greater number of categories. Detailed revisions were made in the light of these suggestions.

Mapping of the relationship between terms used in different national systems and the simple cross-national categorisation was confirmed as crucial to facilitating international comparisons of special needs data. The issue was raised about whether at the consensus stage there should be a forced choice of national sub-categories into a particular one of the three categories, or whether multiple categorisation would be permissible.

There is a strong federal legislative framework which impinges directly on special needs education in the United States. The general issue raised is that it will be necessary to sensitise questionnaire respondents to the implications of a wide-ranging resource-based definition of special needs in considering the full range of legislation which is relevant.

On barriers and facilitators, financial systems were stressed as being central (*e.g.* value of placement neutral funding formulas). Monitoring of performance/performance evaluation and the publication of performance data were cited. Other suggestions mainly fell under the category of potential data dependent indicators (*e.g.* relative costs of inclusive and segregated placement) rather than systemic features.

Discussion of the availability of data for this exercise confirmed the view from earlier pilot visits that any thorough-going attempt to include a special needs dimension to the general UOE data collection exercise was premature given the lack of availability of data on the majority of the questions that would have to be posed.

This strengthened the developing view that the preferred strategy is to concentrate on a severely limited set of objectives in terms of coverage but to seek to achieve comparability, reliability and validity on a key set of central data linked directly to educational indicators agreed as useful, by probing in depth on definitional matters (*e.g.* in relation to categories of special needs and of resources).

Zambia

The visit involved discussions with representatives of the Planning Unit of the Ministry of Education and of the inspectorate, including the Principal Inspector for Primary Education who has overall responsibility for special needs in the inspectorate.

The discussions focused primarily on the nature of the statistical data on special needs which is currently collected, underlying issues on the interpretation of these data, and what possibilities exist for collecting additional data – particularly in the context of the special study.

There are special schools and special units (based and administered within regular schools) for pupils with special needs in the four categories of physical, mental, visual and hearing impairment. There is some integration of the pupils in the special units into regular classrooms of the schools and a relatively small number of other pupils with acknowledged special needs in regular schools (*e.g.* where resources were not available to set up a special unit).

Most schools are government schools but there are a substantial number set up by other organisations (*e.g.* missionaries) which receive government aid; and of entirely private schools. These include both special schools and special classes. There is also some vocational training for special needs pupils, administered by other ministries.

The Zambian system is highly centralised in several respects, not least in its system of collecting educational statistics. There is an annual data collection exercise which requires all heads of primary schools to submit a return on a standard form, with all heads of secondary schools submitting a very similar return. These cover student numbers, split by gender, by grade and by age. The form has been modified in the last few years to also call for numbers of pupils with special needs in the four categories of physical, mental, visual and hearing impairment – also split by grade and gender. A separate return is made for repeaters – a category which includes those with special needs as above and hence some double counting. Other information is called for about resources, finance, etc., but the only other aspect where there is separable information relating to special needs is in connection with teaching staff. Here whether or not the teacher is special needs trained and the specialism of that training (in the four categories above) is recorded.

In addition to this, the inspectorate collect statistical data but in connection with specific initiatives or inspections rather than on a regular basis. Nevertheless this information provides cross-checks on the national data.

The data are clearly in standard form and substantial efforts have been made to achieve high quality through training sessions and monitoring of any apparently aberrant returns. Nevertheless it is thought that the special needs numbers within schools are somewhat under-reported (*e.g.* by comparison with inspectorate cross-checks) due to a lack of sensitisation of regular school heads to special needs. It is also likely that there is some mis-categorisation and variability of criteria for use of the categories particularly in relation to mental impairment.

The incidence of those with special needs within schools is also thought to be only a relatively small fraction of those who have special needs (in the sense that they would need additional resources to access the curriculum if they were in school) due to a multiplicity of factors (*e.g.* stigma attached to special needs; distance and cost of education).

A pilot project in the Copper Belt is seeking to address issues of identification and assessment particularly in the early years, and to facilitate access to education of those with special needs.

There is a difference between "age" and "school age" in the Zambian school system. The official school starting age is 7 at Grade 1. However parents present children for starting at school (supported by affidavit as to age) both at earlier and later ages. Typical ranges given were between 5-12 years. The phenomenon is substantial with estimates of the percentage of 7-year-olds in Grade 1 being below 50%. This causes statistical confusion, giving for example much higher age participation ratios in education than the true figures. This feature, and others teased out of the statistics, will need to be borne in mind in considering the special needs data in countries where these are similar issues.

The inspectorate were very positively inclined adding to and strengthening their database in special needs. They are already proposing to supplement their census data collection exercise with a series of sample survey exercises with a substantially enhanced range of questions. They were happy to co-operate actively in later stages of the special study. In particular they indicated that they would endeavour to collect data relevant to the questionnaire over and above what they currently collect.

The study visit achieved its prime objective of understanding the special needs statistics currently collected and, by extension, some of the general issues likely to arise in the exercise in relation to developing countries. Visits to a special school, a special unit, and the college which trains the overwhelming majority of teachers of special needs children in Zambia enabled the information gained to be grounded in the realities of these settings.

It was also felt that the visit was of value in that it clearly lifted the profile of special needs in the planning unit and helped colleagues in the inspectorate to establish the place of special needs within the policy concerns of the Ministry.

Hungary

The visit involved discussions with representatives of the Ministry for Culture and Education. The discussions focused primarily on the nature of the statistical data on special needs which is currently collected, underlying issues on the interpretation of these data, and what possibilities exist for collecting additional data – particularly in the context of the special study.

Meetings with the officer for special education in the Ministry and the Head of the Department of Statistics in the Ministry, were particularly valuable in understanding the legal and financial framework relating to special educational needs, and the type of statistical information available in this field.

Other meetings with representatives of the Department for International Relations in the Ministry, and the Deputy State Secretary responsible for public education assisted in sensitising the Ministry to the existence and nature of the special study, helping to ensure commitment to it both at this stage and later.

The categorisation system used in Hungary is essentially medical and based directly on the WHO system. It was evident that there were likely to be difficulties in adapting this to the resources definition and the cross-national categorisation.

Subsequent analyses of the response received after the visit was of great assistance in helping to clarify and simplify many aspects of the draft instrument.

Flemish Community of Belgium

The visit involved discussions with representatives of the Flemish Ministry for Education, responsible for education in Flanders. Meetings were also attended by representatives from EUROSTAT and DGXXII of the European Commission.

An introduction to the education system in Flanders and to the structure of special education within the system was presented. As in previous visits discussion then focused primarily on the nature of the statistical data on special needs which is currently collected, underlying issues on the interpretation of these data, and what possibilities exist for collecting additional data – particularly in the context of the special study.

There was exhaustive discussion about the resource-based definition of special needs adopted in the study. Concerns were expressed, particularly by the EUROSTAT representative, that such a definition was in danger of including, within the ambit of special needs, types of provision which would not fall within special needs as commonly understood (e.g. provision of additional resources to support first language teaching in Turkish to children of immigrant families in Germany). It was acknowledged that consensus would have to be sought on possible limits to the definition and that this point would have to be addressed explicitly within the questionnaire.

The reverse situation where a special need was acknowledged, but no additional resources provided, was explored (e.g. some children with special needs were integrated into mainstream schools in Flanders). It was agreed that this situation, when combined with the availability of additional resources when such children were in segregated settings, provided a clear example of a barrier to inclusive education in their system.

Clarification was sought by the Flemish representatives as to what is meant by additional resources in the definition, particularly in the context of a system where the regular classroom already has a very favourable staff-student ratio. This highlighted an interesting area calling for further consideration.

The draft instrument and its annexes were used to structure the discussion and a wide range of useful details were made. The Flemish educational system has a well-defined set of types of special needs which appear to be capable of mapping onto the simple categorisation with only minor difficulties. Generally speaking it appears that the quality of data relating to their segregated provision is good and the representatives involved were familiar with the UOE data collection exercise and its conventions.

The amount of integrated provision is relatively small, although important, and acknowledged as something which should be fostered. Reservations were expressed about the extent to which worthwhile data could be obtained in this context but the colleagues concerned were interested in this aspect and ready to explore possibilities.

In general it was clear that the Flemish representatives were actively supportive of the project and were seeking an informed understanding of the aims and approach of the special study to facilitate their contribution to it.

Sri Lanka

The programme was organised by the Director of Education in the Special Education Unit of the Ministry of Education and Higher Education. The visit included discussions with representatives of the Ministry of Education and Higher Education including the Director of Education in the Special Education Unit, representatives of the statistics section of the Ministry, members of the Department of Special Education of the Sri Lankan National Institute of Education, the Director of Social Services for Sri Lanka, and the national co-ordinator for SHIA (the Swedish Organisation of the Handicapped International Aid Foundation).

Adjoining special schools for the blind and the deaf at Ratmalana in Colombo were visited during which there were discussions with the two Principals. There was also a visit to the Sabaragamuwa Provincial Implementation Unit and Resource Centre which served a rural region on the edge of the hill country in central Sri Lanka. The centre is part of the Primary School Development Plan and was provided and supported by the Swedish overseas aid organisation (SIDA), who have mounted a series of pilot programmes on various aspects of primary schooling from the centre. A nine day residential in-service training for primary teachers to handle children with special needs was taking place. This provided an opportunity for a lively discussion of issues concerning special needs education in rural communities including the collection of reliable statistical data.

Education is clearly regarded as a priority in Sri Lanka which is noteworthy given their lack of resources and the large amount of the economy (over 20%) which is devoted to the continuing conflict with Tamil separatists in the north of the island. Figures of over 90% of 5-year-olds in school and over 75% of the 5-18 year age range in school are claimed (although these probably represent maximum figures of those who have attended for part of the year). The average pupil/teacher ratio is in the low twenties and an absence of gender differences in school enrolments is a marked feature, with actually more girls than boys in the higher classes studying for the British general certificate of secondary education at advanced level (GCSE A-level). The large proportion of females in positions of responsibility was also in marked contrast to that noted in some of the study visits.

There is currently an extremely complex and detailed statistical database with head count data minutely sub-categorised for each of the over 4.5 million school pupils. Four sub-categories of special need are recognised – blind and visually handicapped; deaf and partially hearing; mentally disabled; and physically handicapped. Numbers considered to fall under these categories are currently available for all classes of all schools. The mentally disabled are categorised on the basis of a decision by the class teacher; numbers in other sub-categories derive from a medical decision. The figures for mentally disabled in ordinary schools are considered to be dubious, as to date, little guidance has been given to teachers on this.

The statistics section is run by a person from a central Census and Statistics Office who is seconded out to the Ministry of Education. A useful feature is that all schools of whatever kind are required by law to complete the statistical returns, and non-compliance is unheard of. Unfortunately from the point of view of the special study the current data collection exercise is to be severely curtailed as from 1997 and data will only be generally gathered at class level. It is also proposed to drop the collection of information about categories of special needs. This will lead to the disappearance of special needs information other than for the special schools. However, in the short term, reasonable extrapolations from the 1993-96 data should be possible. There is also the possibility that head count data will continue to be collected for year 1 (5-year-olds), year 6 and A-level classes.

A major issue from the point of view of the definition of special needs adopted in the special study is that it appears that pupils categorised as having special needs in ordinary schools (apart from those in special classes) often do not have additional resources. There is some provision of hearing aids for partially hearing pupils but waiting lists are of the order of years. Otherwise the only discernible additional resource is in-service teacher training. Special schools and special classes do fall within the definition as, *inter alia*, they have significantly smaller pupil/teacher ratios.

Substantial contributions to the education of those with special needs are made by various NGOs (*e.g.* the two Swedish organisations mentioned above) and it would appear to be difficult to gather information about some of their work, particularly as some of them are known to be averse to the collection of statistical information.

While private education in Sri Lanka is rare, the special schools are all private but with some government support. This is mainly to cover teachers' salaries, from the Ministry of Education, and residential accommodation, from the Department of Social Services. All other monies have to be found by their Board of Governors and can be from a wide variety of sources, primarily religious in nature.

The Ministry advocates integration and inclusive education. The great majority of those categorised as falling within the four sub-categories are in normal schools. This appears to be integration in the geographical sense, with little or no additional resources flowing from the categorisation.

The special units in ordinary schools seem to have arisen when there are concentrations of categorised children in a school and it has not proved possible to set up a special school nearby. They have a more favourable pupil/teacher ratio than the regular class (however there could be statistical problems where specialist teachers cover units in four or five schools and multiple counting may occur).

Widely varying opinions were given as to the proportion of pupils with special needs within the categories who were not identified and/or not attending school. Estimates ranged from 10% (*i.e.* the same proportion as not attending in the population overall) to up to 80% in rural areas (where it was suggested that many parents would prefer not to reveal that they had a child with disability or would not understand the concept of disability – particularly in relation to mental disability, partial vision or hearing).

The only other area of special need outside their four categories suggested in several discussions was that of rural communities. Interestingly a major problem was seen as the very small single teacher school often with highly favourable pupil/teacher ratios but with no facilities and an untrained teacher was seen as a major problem. Staff at the National Institute recognised other categories such as learning difficulties and behavioural problems and sought to provide training resources to help teachers in these areas. However they are not covered by statistics.

As a developing country with a high value placed on education Sri Lanka is clearly finding great difficulty in providing additional resources for all but a few of the pupils recognised as having special needs. There are a number of interesting initiatives but they appear to reach only a tiny proportion of those in need. Bearing their system in mind will be of considerable value in avoiding misinterpretation of statistics for developing countries.

Netherlands

The visit involved discussions with representatives of the Netherlands Ministry of Education, Culture and Science. It was notable for the wide range of persons involved covering several different policy making and analysis fields relevant to special needs, as well as central finance, data collection, statistical and information systems specialists. It was particularly helpful that several of these persons had strong links with OECD and the indicators work as well as with other international bodies.

Prior to the meetings Dutch representatives had responded to the pre-circulated draft instrument and had prepared an agenda covering what they considered as the main issues arising from their completion of the instrument. This detailed response to the instrument covered virtually all the factual points relating to the availability or otherwise of statistical information about the Dutch system relevant to the concerns of the special study. An "Information Document" on the structure of the Dutch education system (prepared by the EURYDICE Unit; revised in 1996) was also made available and provided very useful contextual information as well as some specific data on the organisation of special needs education.

There was, as on several other visits, extensive discussion about the resource-based definition of special needs adopted in the study. Concerns were expressed, particularly by a representative with university affiliations, about the possible circularity of such a definition and its lack of a theoretical rationale. It was also suggested that rather than providing a definition in terms of the provision of additional resources, it might be preferable to lead with those having particular difficulties in accessing the regular curriculum. While the force of such comments was acknowledged it was accepted generally that the requirement was for an operational definition which was helpful in terms of administrative requirements and the needs of planners of educational systems.

In the absence of viable alternative suggestions consensus was achieved in going forward along the lines proposed in the instrument, but with a commitment to review the progress made by so doing.

Exploration of the implications of following the resource-based definition followed. Likely problems in obtaining valid and reliable data, which could be meaningfully compared across national systems, were pointed out and accepted. While there was some advocacy of epidemiological approaches adopting agreed international definitions (e.g. in the context of specific organic disorders) the impossibility of proceeding in this way for the present study was generally accepted, as was the inescapable dependence on pre-existing statistics as already collected nationally.

The importance of the mapping exercise linking national categories to the simple tri-partite categorisation proposed in the study was accepted and the specifics of doing this in the Dutch context discussed. Generally this was seen as non-problematic providing that agreement was achieved on conventions for dealing with issues such as a national category mapping to more than one of the simple categories (with support for an approach which made a single allocation to what was regarded as the most central or important category). It was notable that as the discussions proceeded there was a growing ease with which the simple categories were used and the translation done from the Dutch categorisation without apparent difficulty.

The general impression gained was of a well-developed statistical system which was able to cope with the likely range of questions to be incorporated in the questionnaire. It appeared that better financial information was available than had been the case on most other visits, although a general problem was the lack of any central information on the monies and other resources which go into education from non-government sources. Some estimation would be needed but procedures for doing this were already familiar. It was notable, though not surprising, that planners directly involved with special needs were able to vouch for the existence of particular types of data breakdowns which those with more general statistical responsibilities were surprised to find possible.

Suggestions for possible indicators relating to special needs had been put forward in the response to the instrument and were discussed in detail. They were in general realistic in the sense that in their system data are available to support the indicator, and in line with suggestions already received. Specific and idiosyncratic features of the Dutch system were explained and discussed. Notable amongst these were the highly differentiated nature of specialist provision in the special needs field. Substantial changes are in progress (*e.g.* parents can choose between segregated and integrated settings for their children with special needs; and for the money to follow the child to the chosen setting).

Second meeting of national representatives

A further revision of the proposed data collection instrument was presented to a meeting of country representatives (plus representation from DGXXII of the European Commission and from UNESCO) in November 1997. It was explained that in order to embed the work as fully as possible in the full UOE data collection exercise, the version of the instrument which was pilot tested was designed to provide, as far as possible, a parallel special needs version of the UOE data structure. However, it became clear from the first pre-pilot (amply confirmed on the second pilot) that it was not possible, at this stage, to provide such a version since much of the necessary data was not widely available. Thus what was included in the version presented to the meeting reflected what was seen as both possible and important and was strongly influenced by the information obtained during the course of the field visits.

The instrument described at the end of the text was divided into two parts, a questionnaire and a set of data tables. The first part comprises a questionnaire which asks for mainly qualitative information about special educational needs. A key feature is the resources-based definition of special needs education.

There was further discussion about the implications of using this definition. The definition (in terms of additional resources made available to those with particular difficulties in accessing the regular curriculum) raises a fundamental question as to whether those students with disabilities and/or learning difficulties but for whom no additional resources are available still have special educational needs? This problem emphasises that the concept of special educational needs is not simply another euphemism for disability but one which changes the point of reference. That is, it focuses on the adaptations that the school system must make to meet the needs of the child and not on the within-child impairments. Thus, from the point of view of the education system, it is the relative additional effort it has to make to improve the quality and the outcomes for those with special educational needs within the context of providing an efficient education for all children which becomes the key policy concerns, and it is these positive developments which the resource-based definition is trying to highlight.

A second key feature, which obtained very substantial support in the pilot work, is the adoption of a classification scheme which affords countries the opportunity to reinterpret their data in a way that would allow for international comparisons to be made. To achieve this, a tri-partite scheme has been developed. This provides three categories. As indicated earlier, Category A refers to the educational needs of students where there is substantial normative agreement concerning the nature of the special need – such as blind and partially sighted, deaf and partially hearing. Category B refers to educational needs of students who have difficulties in learning which do not appear to be directly or primarily attributable to factors which would lead to categorisation as either A or C. And Category C, which refers to educational needs of students which are considered to arise mainly from socio-economic and/or linguistic factors, *i.e.* where some sort of disadvantage is perceived to be present. It was stressed that it was up to countries to choose into which of categories A, B or C they placed their own national categories.

The second part of the instrument comprises a set of data collection tables which asks for quantitative data in the form of readily available statistics about national educational systems in relation to special educational needs.

An extensive discussion at the meeting touched on a wide variety of issues. In general terms the complexity and difficulty of the task was well recognised and many representatives commented on its potential usefulness. The secretariat received considerable praise for the work completed. Most countries noted that despite the fact that the instrument, quite inevitably, raised problems of both a conceptual and technical nature they did not feel that these were insurmountable and that they would be able to provide relevant information and to complete some, if not all, of the data tables. The view was expressed that the instrument should be concise and that all the data provided should be useful, usable and used in the reporting of the work and the construction of indicators.

The main areas where revisions were required included additional clarification to the use of Categories A, B and C; and in particular where children with behaviour difficulties, the gifted and those with multiple handicaps would fit. Further description was needed on the classification of those who act as teachers in special education since many of them are not necessarily trained as teachers. The link between institutions and categories of special needs was also seen as requiring further exploration, since they do not necessarily map onto each other in any direct way. In addition, it was noted that there are other forms of institutional provision that exist to cope with low incidence handicapping conditions which should be considered. The division of the questionnaire into primary and secondary sections was suggested along with a number of technical points concerned with avoiding overlap and repetition of data gathered. The addition of information in the areas of the social services that support schools (*e.g.* parent education programmes) was suggested.

Additions to the introduction were proposed that would provide an account of the limits of the study with respect to the current data requests vis-à-vis the remainder of the UOE exercise. For instance during the field studies it became clear that data pertaining to the post-compulsory period were not readily available and there was a strong view that for the time being at least this age period should not be further explored. Other areas of importance which needed further consideration included issues relating to violence, truancy drop out and unemployment. Providing some vision of how the study could be expanded in the future for example by including these areas was suggested. Furthermore the value of the study as a formative exercise for developing effective special education provision should also be stressed.

Inevitably the developments outlined in the paragraph above would expand the size of the instrument which some already felt was large enough. It was eventually agreed to proceed with the current version (further modified in line with the comments made) and to incorporate additional issues when the first data gathering round was completed.

There was considerable discussion on the type of indicators that would be useful. Indicators which would be available if the current instrument were completed comprised: numbers and proportions of those with special educational needs; the location of their education; teacher/pupil ratios; relative resourcing; and system features relating to obstacles and facilitators to integration. Other indicators were identified during discussion. These included: the expected years of schooling; equity in terms of gender and ethnic minority issues; systems indicators *e.g.* linking school organisation to behaviour problems; and partnerships.

In addition there was great interest in the development of outcome indicators particularly with reference to the contexts of education; achievement; costs; quality of education; the link to post-compulsory placement; employment; the link between inclusion and outcomes for those children without special educational needs; and the costs of policies of not integrating students with special needs.

The countries agreed to take part in a wider field testing of the questionnaire. It was agreed that this sample should include those countries present at the meeting, plus a number of others to be identified. In addition the representatives from UNESCO agreed to include up to 10 other countries making a sample of approximately 30 countries in all. It was agreed that data from the year 1995/96 should as far as possible be used.

It was also agreed that the instrument should be revised in the light of the discussion and be re-circulated for completion at the beginning of 1998. The countries present would endeavour to return completed forms as soon as possible with the intention of reviewing the information and data thus obtained at a meeting in the summer of 1998.

Field testing of the instrument

The instrument was circulated to all OECD countries and to a number of developing countries. This latter part of the exercise was undertaken by UNESCO and will be reported separately under their aegis at a later date. Analysis of the responses from OECD countries forms the main empirical basis for this monograph as developed in the following chapters.

A report based on the first ten responses which had been received by the beginning of June 1998 was presented to a third meeting of country representatives in July 1998. An earlier presentation was made at the meeting of the INES Technical Group at The Hague, Netherlands 27-29 April 1998 on the Special Study in Special Educational Needs giving an indication of the approach taken and the type of data which will result from the present exercise. There was a full discussion of the issues involved and an interest in including information arising from the pilot data collection exercise in the 1998 edition of *Education at a Glance*.

Following discussion at the INES Technical Group meeting in July 1998, agreement was reached for the analysis of the first set of responses to be included in this edition of *Education at a Glance* (OECD, 1998, pp. 221-229). A fuller data set has also been reported in *Education at a Glance* (see OECD, 2000, Indicator C6, p. 187).

It was very encouraging to note that completion of the questionnaire and data collection tables, while difficult, was regarded as feasible by representatives involved in widely differing types of educational systems ranging from largely integrated to largely segregated, and from both categorical and non-categorical-based systems. The use of a resource-based definition of special educational needs appeared to achieve a high degree of acceptance.

Further discussion of the findings from the exercise and their implications is provided in the following chapters.

Chapter 3

QUALITATIVE DATA ANALYSIS

Background

Apart from gathering quantitative data, countries were asked to provide some qualitative descriptions. These comprised:

- information on the country's definition of special education used for gathering educational statistics;

- the use of categories in gathering data in this field along with the names and definitions of the categories and whether or not they fall within the resources definition;

- whether there were categories of students currently used for data collection which fall within the resources definition but not within the national definition of special needs;

- whether the resources provided were substantial or minimal;

- how the categories fit into the cross-national categorisation A, B and C;

- if there are no categories, how planning decisions are made for students with special educational needs;

- whether there is specific coverage of special educational needs in the current legislative framework and if so what it is;

- factors considered to be facilitators of inclusion and equity; and factors acting as barriers to inclusion and equity.

Replies to these questions are synthesised in the following paragraphs based on returns from 23 OECD Member countries: Austria, Belgium (Flemish Community), Canada (New Brunswick), the Czech Republic, Denmark, France, Finland, Germany, Greece, Hungary, Italy, Ireland, Korea, Mexico, the Netherlands, Portugal, New Zealand, Spain, Sweden, Switzerland, Turkey, the United Kingdom and the United States.

Laws

All countries surveyed have laws covering special education provision or they are in preparation. It is an area where there is substantial development. Most countries run both regular and special schools and use categorical systems of classification for allotting additional resources, and some provide guidelines determining the content of teacher training programmes. The most significant development in these legal frameworks is a move towards inclusion which is being driven by an agenda comprising human rights issues, parental involvement, social cohesion and the growing understanding that the concept of special educational needs implies that students' failures to make adequate progress in their learning are in large part the responsibility of the school and cannot be viewed as being caused wholly by the "disability" attributed.

The changes in thinking are reflected, for instance, in the Netherlands where the WPO (New Primary Education Act, 1998), incorporates the statutory provisions of special schools for children with learning and behavioural difficulties, and children with learning difficulties and pre-school children with developmental difficulties with regular primary schools as special schools for primary education. Parallel arrangements for older students will come into force with a Secondary Educational Act and expertise found in other types of special school will be brought together under a new Expertise Centres Act.

The interactive compensatory view of special educational needs has in some countries led to an expansion of the numbers of students under consideration to include those with disadvantages. In Denmark and Spain the term "special education requirements" is used and reflects the fact that many students will need a flexible approach to engender achievement. Furthermore, for instance in Mexico, it is importantly recognised that some disabled students may not have special educational needs. This follows from the observation that if certain disabilities are being skilfully handled in a school as part of the regular provision additional help to access the curriculum is not needed.

The recognition that schools must adapt themselves is being reflected in other modifications to educational delivery. Where special needs students are included class sizes are sometimes reduced. In Hungary, for example, a student with special needs counts as three non-special needs students. So a class of 16, comprising two special needs students and 14 others would be equivalent to a class of 20 all non-special needs. To help regular schools adapt, outreach from special schools to regular schools is encouraged as is the development of clusters of schools. The aim here is to help develop the necessary skills in the regular schools so that those with special needs can be more effectively educated there. This approach has been described more fully elsewhere *e.g.* in Canada, New Brunswick (OECD, 1999*a*).

Many countries also offer an extension in age of formal education for disabled students. In New Zealand this can extend from the under 5 to the age of 21.

The significance of parental involvement is widely recognised especially in the assessment arrangements. But more and more parents are being given the right for their disabled child to be educated in regular schools as for instance in Italy (see OECD, 1999*a*).

Facilitators and barriers of equity and inclusive education

Countries were asked to identify characteristics of their educational systems which they believe act as either facilitators or barriers to equity and inclusive education.

Given the diversity of systems involved it is not surprising that answers covered a wide range of topics from the legal system to the practicalities of assessment.

Many countries commented on the importance that legal and policy frameworks may have to encourage inclusion or to create barriers. Compulsory free education for all children and youth, and mandated integration in one country, were identified as obvious facilitators. If children are not in the system they can hardly be included! One identified the opportunities provided by the EU Helios programme on the inclusion of disabled students into mainstream schools as being especially helpful in achieving changes in attitudes and practices.

This relatively straightforward position may however be contrasted with other complex effects which appear when policies are put into practice. In Austria for instance, the abolition of statements of special needs for some students, guaranteeing certain forms of provision, were found to be a barrier to effective education of disabled students since without them they were obliged to follow the regular aims of the school. In addition, regular schools provided two years less required education than special schools. In contrast in the Flemish part of Belgium, the stigmatising effects of assessment and a heavy bureaucratic approach were identified as barriers to inclusion.

Funding of special education was also identified as a key factor. The creation of a level playing field for funding which does not bias placement decisions was seen as an important facilitator. In some countries *e.g.* Denmark, Finland, Hungary and New Zealand, funds follow students and not schools and this opens the way to inclusive practices. A paradox emerged with regard to the decentralisation of the special educational needs grant. While central control was viewed as a barrier to inclusion and decentralisation seen as an important way to help local authorities implement relevant inclusionary policies, decentralisation in the form of the local management of schools in New Zealand was seen as a barrier. A general lack of funds and bias in funding formulae were both perceived to be barriers.

The structure of the school system itself was also identified. The existence of pre-schools and special classes and special schools and a continuum of placement possibilities and links between special and mainstream schools were viewed as facilitators.

Other aspects of structure were seen as barriers. These included, a shorter period of education for regular students, in contrast to that available for those with disabilities, and the structure of primary education itself. At the classroom level, class size and streaming or tracking were seen as barriers. The lack of specialists and the proper use of teachers' aides were seen to be obstacles to be overcome. On the positive side, the addition of extra teachers was a facilitator presumably because they bring additional skills to the classroom, allow for joint planning and lead to a reduction in pupil/teacher ratio in classes where disabled students are included.

In terms of pedagogy, curriculum differentiation and the use of information and communication technology (ICT) were viewed as favourable.

The involvement of other services was seen as facilitating, while difficulties in accessing them as a barrier. Some countries also noted the positive use of research *e.g.* for evaluating systems.

The involvement of parents as advocates facilitated inclusion but the lack of parental involvement and knowledge were viewed as barriers.

Finally a major problem exists around the training of staff. Basic training and in-service education and training (INSET) were viewed as essential and the obverse aspects of negative attitudes on the part of teachers and the lack of relevant training as barriers. Some countries pointed to the split in universities between education and special education as a further constraint.

The existence of educational priority policy and non-discriminatory equal opportunities were also important in the fight for equity and deliberately balancing the numbers of ethnic minorities in schools was seen as a positive equity measure.

Definition of special education for gathering statistics

Based on the returns from the 23 countries participating, the definition of special education for the purposes of gathering national statistics may be grouped into four basic patterns:

- First, there are those countries, for instance the Czech Republic, France and Germany, which collect data via disability categories (always remembering that the term disability itself has no common meaning across countries and in France two systems, emanating from two ministries, operate in parallel);

- Second, there are those such as Greece, Switzerland and New Zealand, which additionally include disadvantaged students. Additionally, some countries such as Switzerland include children with a foreign first language within these categories whilst others do not.

- Third there are those *e.g.* Spain and Turkey which also include gifted students.

- The fourth approach *e.g.* Canada (New Brunswick), is to base provision on the need to respond to exceptionalities leading to perceived difficulties in the schooling process rather than defining students per se via a categorical approach. The data are summarised in Table 3.1.

Table 3.1. **Definition of special education for gathering statistics**

Patterns	AUT	BEL (Fl.)	CAN (NB)	CZE	DNK	FRA	FIN	DEU	GRC	HUN	ITA	IRL	KOR	MEX	NLD	PRT	NZL	ESP	SWE	CHE	TUR	UKM	USA
1	x	x	x	x		x	x	x		x	x		x		x	x							x
2									*x			*x					x			*x			
3																	x				x		
4			x		x									x					x				x

1 = Disability categories only.

2 = Disability categories plus disadvantaged students including * Learning difficulties linked to linguistic barriers or disadvantage associated with ethnic groupings.

3 = Disability categories plus disadvantaged students plus gifted.

4 = Essentially non categorical systems.

Use of categories

The figures show that most countries gather data by means of categories and this question invited them to provide the names of the categories and their definitions. If they did not use categories, they were invited to indicate how planning decisions for special educational needs are made in their countries.

Some countries were able to provide definitions although many were not, and the outcomes are provided in Table 3.2 which reveals the complexity of the different arrangements. In this table the national categories have been placed into cross-national categories A, B and C according to the classifications provided by the countries themselves as requested. Definitions of the categories are also provided where available. In addition, those categories which receive additional resources but which are not part of the national special needs category are indicated by numbers (4.1, 4.2, etc.). A detailed discussion based on national categories is provided in Chapter 4.

Twelve of the 23 countries report having categories which receive additional resourcing but which lie outside their national definition of special needs. These tend to cover disadvantaged students, those from ethnic minorities, those with short-term learning problems and those with specific learning difficulties. However, some countries include gifted students, those with mild behaviour problems and those with speech impairments. These categories of provision exist in other countries too, but in those countries they will be included under the general rubric of special education.

A small number of countries do not fit this classification and fit into the fourth pattern noted above. This approach deserves further comment. The Canadian Province of New Brunswick does not keep categorical data but does have categories which receive resources but are not part of the special needs framework. The United Kingdom does not gather data by categories and in 1995/96 could identify no further resources being made available for students without statements. Denmark also has a non-categorical system but makes a distinction between students with more extensive special needs (being about 1% who have the most severe disabilities and who need extensive support with their learning) and those with less extensive needs (being about 12% and includes those with disadvantages), a framework which is conceptually similar to that in the United Kingdom. Resourcing arrangements for these two groups are different. In these three countries resources are made available for the increased costs which arise in educating students with special educational needs, but they are allotted through local decision-making structures.

OECD 2000

Substantial or minimal resources

Recognising that information on funding for special needs is difficult to obtain (a conclusion supported by the lack of data provided in the relevant question on the instrument), countries were also asked whether they provided substantial or minimal resources for those students with special needs or those receiving additional resources. Of the 16 countries replying, all countries, with the exception of Turkey, indicated that substantial resources were made available for those with disabilities within national category systems. Minimal resources were reported as being provided by five countries. The categories covered were, gifted, specific learning difficulties, refugee children, hearing impaired, autistic, moderate speech or behaviour problems, truancy, English for speakers of foreign languages and targeted funding for educational achievement. In the system adopted by New Zealand the special education grant and funds for resource teachers working in learning and behaviour problem areas were also reported as minimal.

Although this question has self-evident limitations, it does provide some indication that countries see themselves as putting considerable extra effort into this area even though assessing the exact extent is difficult. This issue is addressed later in the monograph where a proxy, in terms a more favourable teacher/student ratio, is used to indicate the degree of additional resources involved.

Cross-national classification

Countries were asked to carry out the task of re-classifying their categories both national and resource-based according to the cross-national model described in Chapter 1. Briefly, cross-national Category A refers to those students whose special needs appear to stem from a clear biological impairment such as deafness or severe learning difficulty. CNC C comprises those whose difficulties stem more apparently from social disadvantage of one sort or another and CNC B covers those who fit clearly neither CNC A nor C.

To complete the task it was suggested that 10 knowledgeable persons be asked to carry out the re-classification and that the resulting decisions should then be summarised. In fact only four countries completed the task as requested although most countries provided a classification.

Countries seemed to have little difficulty in using this framework and the results are summarised in Table 3.2 which shows that most categories were placed as might be expected.

Table 3.2 reveals that the majority of countries use categories to classify their special needs population for the purposes of statistical data gathering. In terms of national categories, i.e. excluding those that additionally fall into the resources definition, they vary between a single category, e.g. the United Kingdom and 19 in Switzerland. Between these extremes many countries use 12 or 13. Although the categories used cover broadly similar disabling conditions, in many countries unavailability of the actual definitions in use render comparisons difficult. For instance, in regard to students with learning difficulties as far as cross-national comparisons are concerned, it is not possible to distinguish between students who would appear under the various headings of severe learning difficulties, moderate learning difficulties, light learning difficulties and learning disabilities. Some countries gather data on students who are blind or have visual impairment separately, others group them together, and similarly for those with serious or partial hearing impairments.

Students with emotional and behavioural problems represent an interesting case. In Greece, Hungary, Italy and Turkey there is no such category. In Austria, Ireland and New Zealand several levels of the category are described.

In terms of the way these national categories are allotted into cross-national categories A, B and C there is general consistency with students with traditional impairments being placed in A and those from disadvantaged backgrounds in C. However, other interesting observations may be made. Students classified as having learning disabilities as well as slow learners often appear in B, i.e. the reasons for difficulties with school learning are unclear, being neither due to disadvantage nor a clear impairment. Those with behaviour problems usually appear under A but in Ireland, Finland, New Zealand and the United States they appear under B, perhaps implying different causal understanding among countries.

This discussion of the results of the findings on national categories and the way they are allotted to the cross-national categories A, B and C strongly supports the rationale of the present study. That is, if meaningful international comparisons are to be made, a method such as the one developed here, which includes all children receiving additional resources, and their allotment into straightforward and operationally defined categories substantially simplifies the situation and improves the possibility of making policy-relevant decisions based on internationally valid comparisons.

Concluding comments

In general terms the qualitative data gathered during the study reveals the great national interest in this area as laws, policies and educational provision are adjusted to meet the needs of students who are failing in the regular system. Factors thought to be facilitators or barriers for equity and inclusion cover a whole range of factors which include legal frameworks, funding models, assessment arrangements, school structure, class size, individual teaching programmes, involvement of additional teachers and aides, teacher training, parental involvement and co-operation with other services. Together these make a substantial agenda for reform.

The next three chapters examine in detail the quantitative data gathered.

Table 3.2. **Allocation of categories of students with disabilities, difficulties, disadvantages included in the resources definition to cross-national categories A, B, C**

	Cross-national category A	Cross-national category B	Cross-national Category C
Austria	2 **Physical disabilities** 3 **Speech disorders** 4 **Hearing impaired children** 5 **Deaf children** 6 **Visually impaired children** 7 **Blind children** 8 **Emotional/behavioural problems** 9 **Moderate or severe mental retardation** 10 **Children with multiple disabilities** 11 **Schools in hospitals** NO DEFINITIONS OF CATEGORIES CURRENTLY MADE AVAILABLE *(see endnote to the table)*	1 **Learning disabilities**	12 **(4.1) Children with specific or subject related learning difficulties (e.g. Dyslexia)** 13 **(4.2) Children with moderate speech problems** 14 **(4.3) Children with moderate behavioural problems**
Belgium (Flemish Community)	1 **Type 1 – Minor mental handicap** *This category is followed by pupils with a minor mental handicap. This type of special education is not organised in nursery school (e.g. this type of education is only organised on primary and secondary level).* 2 **Type 2 – Moderate or serious mental handicap** *This category is followed by pupils with a moderate or serious mental handicap.* 3 **Type 3 – Serious emotional and/or behavioural problems** *This category is followed by pupils with serious emotional and/or behavioural problems.* 4 **Type 4 – Pupils with a physical handicap** *This category is followed by pupils with a physical handicap.* 5 **Type 5 – Children suffering from protracted illness** *This category is followed by pupils suffering from protracted illness.* *Students are in the so-called "hospital schools" for a limited period of time; in the meantime they remain also registered in their regular school.* 6 **Type 6 – Visual handicap** *This category is followed by pupils with a visual handicap.*	14 **(4.2) Extending care** *For a few years now the Flemish Government has been developing a programme for "zorgbreedte" (extending care). It is rather difficult to translate this notion. The idea is linked up with ideas on e.g. "inclusive education". The idea is to organise early attention for those children who might suffer from learning difficulties that may cause problems in the transition between pre-school and primary school. Additional teachers, schools for special education, and the PMS Centres work closely together with the pre-school teacher. Attention is given to general language proficiency, social skills, self-control, and socio-economic problems. The target group consists of children who live in less favourable economic and cultural circumstances but who are capable of participating in ordinary education when certain deficits are eliminated.*	15 **(4.3) Educational priority policy** *The languages of the migrant population are not legally recognised as minority languages. Nevertheless, a special policy has been instituted within the education system to provide for adequate learning opportunities, especially for children within compulsory education. This policy is called the "onderwijsvoorrangsbeleid" (educational priority policy). It is applied at the primary and secondary levels in municipalities with a significant number of migrant or refugee children. Two main lines of action are presented. First, there is a school agreement that promotes equal representation of these children in all schools of a region (at the secondary level this is not always possible because not all courses of study are available or organised in every school). Second, special attention is given, to the quality of the teaching of Dutch as well as to the teaching of the native language and culture of the pupils involved. Extra teaching periods are provided to the schools for the realisation of this project.* 16 **(4.4) Reception classes for pupils who do not speak Dutch** *Reception education is education for immigrant school entrants who do not speak Dutch. Its aim is to insure their knowledge of Dutch and to facilitate their social integration. After reception education, the pupils can enrol in regular education (primary or secondary level). Reception education encourages the active integration of the immigrant school entrants in school life. The focus lies on the relationship with the teachers and the other pupils of*

Table 3.2. **Allocation of categories of students with disabilities, difficulties, disadvantages included in the resources definition to cross-national categories A, B, C** (*cont.*)

	Cross-national category A	Cross-national category B	Cross-national Category C
Belgium (Flemish Community)	**7 Type 7 – Auditory handicap** *This type of special education is for pupils with an auditory handicap.* **8 Type 8 – Serious learning disabilities** *This type of special education is organised for pupils with serious learning disabilities.* *This type of education is only organised at primary level (not for nursery school or secondary education).* **9 Training form 1** *At special secondary education level, four training forms are organised. Pupils from different education types (see categories 1-8) can be gathered. Each education form meets well-determined needs.* *Training form 1 offers social training with the aim of integration into a protected environment. This track can be organised for types of special education 2, 3, 4, 6 and 7 and lasts for at least four years.* **10 Training form 2** *Training form 2 offers general and social training with the aim of integration into a protected environment and work situation. The training lasts for at least four years and is divided into two phases. Vocational training courses outside the school are also organised. This track can be organised for types of special education 2, 3, 4, 6, and 7.* **11 Training form 3** *Training form 3 offers general, social and vocational training with the aim of integration into a regular environment and work situation.* *It can be organised for types of special education 1, 3, 4, 6 and 7. The training is comparable with standard vocational education and lasts five years.* **12 Training form 4** *Training form 4 offers preparation for study in higher education and integration into active life. Training form 4 provides secondary education similar to the general, technical, vocational or an artistic curriculum of mainstream full-time secondary education and is also structured in the same way. The pupils follow the programme mainstream education under the condition that the educational methods are provided which are adapted to*		*his peer group. In elementary education schools with at least four foreign pupils who do not speak Dutch ("anderstalige nieuwkomers") and who do not fully understand the language used at school, a special language adaptation course can be organised for three periods a week. In secondary education this type of education is organised in 14 selected schools. This scheme to improve the integration of migrant children was reinforced by the Decree of 6 April 1992. In applying these measures, 36 priority education areas have been recognised. In these areas, which have high concentrations of immigrants, educational efforts are being intensified in order to eliminate the educational gap at school. The educational system must strive with equal intensity to integrate the immigrants into society; it does so by taking their own language and culture into account and by promoting integration through intercultural education. The attention paid to teaching Dutch, the language of instruction, is crucial in the approach taken by the "Vlaamse Gemeenschap" (Flemish Community). This is why special classes and special opportunities are provided for pupils who attend school but have not yet mastered the Dutch language. In order for these intensified efforts to achieve their intended effect, the number of staff members in schools with many immigrants has considerably increased. Additional counselling and assistance are being provided as well.*

Table 3.2. **Allocation of categories of students with disabilities, difficulties, disadvantages included in the resources definition to cross-national categories A, B, C** (*cont.*)

	Cross-national category A	Cross-national category B	Cross-national Category C
Belgium (Flemish Community)	*their special educational needs or that the time to acquire the programme can be extended as required. It can be organised for types of special education 3, 4, 5, 6, and 7.* 13 **(4.1) Integrated education** *Integrated education (GON) is meant to guide and help handicapped children or youngsters in a regular school with the aid of specialists from special education Handicapped children or children with learning difficulties can go to regular schools permanently or temporarily, part-time or full-time. Additional teaching periods or additional resources are foreseen to realise such an integration.*		
Canada (New Brunswick)	**Behavioural exceptionalities** 1 Communicational 2 3 Intellectual 4 Physical 5 Perceptual 6 Multiple **NO DEFINITIONS OF CATEGORIES CURRENTLY MADE AVAILABLE** **No data for Canada. Allocation to CNC made by the OECD Secretariat.**		7 **(4.1) Gifted** 8 **(4.2) Immigrant** 9 **(4.3) At-risk youth**
Czech Republic	1 **Mentally retarded** 2 **Hearing handicaps** 3 **Sight handicaps** 4 **Speech handicaps** 5 **Physical handicaps** 6 **Multiple handicaps** 7 **Sick lying in hospitals** 8 **Devel. Behaviour and learning problems** 9 **Other handicaps** 10 **With weakened health (kindergarten only)** **NO DEFINITIONS OF CATEGORIES CURRENTLY MADE AVAILABLE**		
Finland	2 **Moderate mental impairment (MOMI)** *This type of comprehensive school education is arranged for students with moderate mental impairment.*	1 **Mild mental impairment (MIMI)** *Adjusted education is arranged for students with mild mental impairment.*	9 **(4.1) Immigrants** *This type of education is provided to immigrants who first are involved in preparatory education and after that in special or regular education.*

Table 3.2. **Allocation of categories of students with disabilities, difficulties, disadvantages included in the resources definition to cross-national categories A, B, C** (cont.)

	Cross-national category A	Cross-national category B	Cross-national Category C
Finland	3 **Hearing impairment (HI)** *The education is provided for students with a hearing defect for deaf and blind and for dysphasia students, especially when sign language is needed.* 4 **Visual impairment (VI)** *Provided for students with various kinds of visual defects.* 5 **Physical & other impairment (POHI)** *This type of education is provided to students whose learning difficulties are due to a neurological defect or developmental disorder (such as the MBD syndrome) or a motoric handicap (such as the CP).* 7 **Others** *This category includes special education for students who have e.g. epilepsy, diabetes or a heart disease and who do not fall into other categories on the basis of their educational needs.*	6 **Emotional & social impairment (EI)** *Education is intended for emotionally disturbed and socially maladjusted students.* 8 **Specific learning disabilities (SLD)** *This part-time special education is provided for pupils suffering from speech, reading writing and other specific difficulties or who have subject specific learning difficulties.* 10 **(4.2) Support teaching** *This education is provided to students who are occasionally "behind" in their studies or need special support for some other reason*	
France	1 **Severe mental handicap** *Severe mental handicap (IQ between 20 & 34) concerns persons who can benefit from the systematic learning of simple gestures.* 2 **Moderate mental handicap** *Moderate mental handicap (IQ between 35 & 49) concerns persons able to acquire simple notions of communication, hygiene and elementary safety as well as simple manual skills, but who are incapable of learning how to do arithmetic or read.* 3 **Mild mental handicap** *This category covers handicaps as regards intelligence, memory and thinking. It concerns persons (IQ between 50 & 70) capable of learning practical skills and how to read, as well as notions of arithmetic thanks to special education, and who can be taught a certain degree of socialisation.* 4 **Physical handicap** *Orthopedic and motor deficiencies have been broadly interpreted as covering the structure of the body and its visible parts. Such handicaps include mechanical and functional alterations to the face, head, neck, trunk and limbs, as well as limbs which are missing in whole or in part.*	15 **(4.2) Remedial classes, special secondary 3rd year classes and 4th year vestibule classes** *Remedial classes are designed for children who for various reasons have learning difficulties at elementary level. Special 3rd year classes and 4th year vestibule classes (second level) provide assistance and support to pupils with problems at school and unable to derive benefit from the general and technical instruction normally given. Together with remedial classes, they form part of the system of assistance, support and insertion.* 17 **(4.4) SEGPA** *SEGPAs (special sections for general or occupational training) are incorporated into public and private secondary schools (usually lower secondary ones). They make it easier for pupils with learning difficulties to pursue their studies.*	14 **(4.1) CLINs & Reception classes** *Initiation classes (CLINs) have been created in primary schools for non-French speaking pupils of foreign nationality. Reception classes, in 1st to 4th year secondary (but mainly 1st year), are offered to foreign pupils (in principle, non-French speaking, newly arrived in France and whose age corresponds to that of the school).* 18 **(4.5) ZEP** *ZEPs (priority education zones) are, for the most part, made up of schools and lower secondary schools, rarely higher secondary schools providing general and technical education. ZEPs are concentrated in the main urban centres.* *Only 10% of ZEP pupils (compared to 30% of non-ZEP ones) live in small towns (of less than 10 000 inhabitants). The geographical distribution of ZEPs reflects in part (but in part only) that of socially and economically deprived areas. The characteristics of ZEP pupils – from disadvantaged backgrounds, and often with severe learning difficulties – are naturally linked to the objectives of this policy.*

Table 3.2. **Allocation of categories of students with disabilities, difficulties, disadvantages included in the resources definition to cross-national categories A, B, C** (*cont.*)

	Cross-national category A	Cross-national category B	Cross-national Category C
France			

5 Metabolic disorders
Metabolic or nutritional disorders include abnormal development and maturation, gluten intolerance diabetes, malnutrition, and weight loss or gain (but exclude thinness and obesity).

6 Deaf
Disorders in this category concern not only the ear but also its ancillary parts and its functions. The most important sub-division is that of hearing impairment. The term "deaf" should only be applied to persons whose hearing impairment is such that it cannot be helped by any hearing aid. Like blindness, deafness is a serious sensory impairment.

7 Partially hearing
Disorders in this category concern not only the ear but also its ancillary parts and functions. The most important sub-division is that of hearing impairment.

8 Blind
Blindness is a serious sensory impairment. Such impairment may be marked (very poor vision or partial blindness), almost total (severe or almost total blindness) or total (no perception of light). It may affect one eye or both.

9 Partially sighted
Other visual impairments include astigmatism, accommodation deficiency, diplopia (strabismus), amblyopia, and sensitivity to light.

10 Other neuropsychological disorders
Neuropsychological disorders have been defined to include any interference with the basic elements of the mental process. This being so, the functions listed are those which normally involve the presence of basic neuropsychological and psychological mechanisms.

11 Speech and language disorders
Speech disorders or impairment include artificial larynx, severe dysarthria, lack of voice expression, and stuttering, while language disorders or impairment include central impairment of the visual function with inability to communicate (e.g. severe dyslexia).

12 Other deficiencies
Other deficiencies are all those not mentioned above.

Table 3.2. **Allocation of categories of students with disabilities, difficulties, disadvantages included in the resources definition to cross-national categories A, B, C** (*cont.*)

	Cross-national category A	Cross-national category B	Cross-national Category C
France	**13 Multiple handicapped** *Children or young people in special educational establishments suffer from a main handicap, which is usually the reason they are attending special classes. But they may suffer from other disorders in addition to this main one.* **16 (4.3) EREA** *EREAs (special regional schools) are second level public schools. They take pupils who would have problems following lessons in normal schools.*		
Germany	**2 Blind** *Children or youth without visual faculty or whose visual faculty is largely impaired resulting in an inability to function like seeing persons (even after an optical correction e.g. glasses).* **3 Partially sighted** *Students having a central visual acuity on the better eye or on both eyes of 0.3 or less for the distance despite a correction by glasses but without other aids; or having a visual acuity of 0.3 (Nieden V) or less for the proximity regarding a working distance of at least 30 centimetres; or whose faculty of vision is impaired to a similar degree despite better visual acuity.* **4 Deaf** *Students who – irrespective of their actual deficiency in hearing capacity – are not capable to notice acoustic signals of their environment and to make use of them for acquiring speech, speech hearing and an active or passive phonetic speech competence.* **5 Partially hearing** *Students who are hearing impaired from a minor to medium degree.* **6 Speech impairment** *Children whose speech and development of speaking is largely impaired so that entry into or stay in a regular school with ambulant school-accompanying promotion programmes (Sprachheilklassen) is regarded as insufficient.* **7 Physically handicapped** *Children who due to their physical handicap, the accompanying disturbances and/or organic defects and illnesses cannot or not sufficiently be promoted in regular schools.*	**1 Students with learning handicaps** *Children or youth needing promotion through special education due to a considerable and long lasting deficiency in learning capacity.* **9 Disturbed in behaviour, conduct** *Children with large psychic disorders and who are socially conspicuous.* **12 Unknown, no information** *Not available.*	

Table 3.2. **Allocation of categories of students with disabilities, difficulties, disadvantages included in the resources definition to cross-national categories A, B, C** (*cont.*)

	Cross-national category A	Cross-national category B	Cross-national Category C
Germany	**8 Mentally handicapped** *not available* **10 Sick** *Children who are being treated in clinics, hospitals or sanatoriums for a longer period of time and who are capable to take part in lessons.* **11 Multiple handicaps** *not available*		
Greece	**1 Blind – partially sighted** *We call blind the students that cannot read printed materials and acquire knowledge through vision. Blind students are educated in special units at primary level and in regular schools at secondary level. We call partially sighted those who can read printed materials with big characters so as to acquire experiences through vision. The educational system insists in using the existing percentage of vision so as to enforce the sensory motor skills and prevent loss of sensations e.g. colour, spatial aptitude and orientation, motion, speech ability, body mobility. Blind students study in special school at secondary level. Partially s ghted students study in mainstream schools and they dc not differ from their seeing peer students. Both blind and partially sighted follow the common core curricula. Flexible curricula are now being prepared for this category so that blind may be integrated in mainstream school.* **2 Deaf – hearing impaired** *Deaf is who, with or without hearing aids, cannot hear any sound. Hearing impaired is who can hardly hear a sound. Discrimination is done between a) those that are born deaf and b) those that became deaf after 3-4 years of age. The first had never acoustic experiences, the second had a period of normal linguistic performance and their problem is not only how to develop speaking but mainly how to safeguard speech acquired. The second are much more privileged than the first. Education gives emphasis to the early diagnosis by a committee consisting of a doctor, audiologist, psychologist, social worker and pedagogue. It is easy to have diagnosis of complete deafness, but hearing impairment often is recognised only when the child enters the kindergarten or pre-school education. The teaching curricula for deaf are common to all mainstream schools, adjusted though to their needs i.e. emphasis is given to language teaching (more time spent), to auditory training, articulation and*	**5 Autistic** *Autistic children may present very or less severe difficulties in behaviour. Development may present unsteadiness unlike mentally retarded who can have more slow but more steady improvement. Autistic students present psychomotor problems, which prevent them from being included in the social environment and the educational system. This category of children was and still is under the administration of the Ministry of Health and Social Affairs, as being hosted in Special Institutions. Recently more and more pupils are accepted in special schools of mentally retarded students because of the Ministry of Education introduced training programmes for autistic children. Within the framework of special education (Pammacaristos scñool in Athens, PIKPA in Ioannina). This policy tries to de-institutionalise this category of special educational needs and introduces programmes with psychomotor objectives in teaching skills i.e. personal care of daily living (feeding, bathing, etc.) at primary level special schools. Furthermore, special software programmes funded by Socrates and Horizon develop pilot applications, which try to help them in space exploration and communicating training (with Bliss or Makaton symbols) in the regular educational environment. Special re-educational programmes for 100 teachers have been planned by the directorate of Special Education within the 2nd European Community framework support, so that they can work with autistic children which will start the next academic year (1998-99).* **6 Learning difficulties** *By learning difficulties we refer to difficulties due to various reasons and factors: pathological, socio-economic, psychological, unfavourable school environment. This category umbrella shelters several sub-categories of learning difficulties, e.g. students with dyslexia (5% in Greece, 1994 data), with behaviour disturbances,*	

Table 3.2. **Allocation of categories of students with disabilities, difficulties, disadvantages included in the resources definition to cross-national categories A, B, C** (cont.)

	Cross-national category A	Cross-national category B	Cross-national Category C
Greece	*phonetics, social rehabilitation. Deaf students are educated in special schools whereas hearing impaired are in mainstream schools.*	*communication disorders, emotional disturbance, neurological disorders, solitary behaviour, rejection due to racial and socio-economic factors, aggressiveness, etc., resulting to social maladjustment and marginalisation.*	
	3 Physically handicapped	*Students follow the common core curriculum but they are provided in parallel outside the school programme, special teaching support in one or more subjects. A special class can be established with decision of the District Educational Authority, the school advisor of special education and the mainstream school unit of the student, according to the Presidential Decrees 603/83 and 472/83. Teachers are expected to have deep knowledge of the learning difficulty, special training in selecting the appropriate pedagogical approach and accuracy in using the methodology needed in every case so as to motivate and help the student towards his/her inclusion in the mainstream class. This is a very demanding post and we should admit that it is not always the case that teachers undertake this difficult task. As a result special classes often offer to students simply an extra time of repetition and not of creativity and awareness.*	
	We call physically handicapped the students who suffer from cerebral palsy, spina bifida, myopathy, etc., and present a mobility handicap. The Greek educational system ought to integrate all those students to regular school units, though a 40% present serious learning difficulties. Repercussions in their education are deriving from speech, memory, thinking, visual neurological impairments. On the other hand the existing special schools units which recruit this category of students follow the common core curriculum of the mainstream schools and focus in rehabilitating and integrating them in a social environment. As a result, the fact that physically handicapped students study in special units (#7 primary and #3 secondary) is a rather strange situation though the offered teaching programmes are common with those of the mainstream schools. In the special units, personnel, such as physiotherapists, ergotherapist, social workers and psychologist support students is specialised. Teachers are specialised at primary level, but no specialisation still exists at secondary level.		
	4 Mentally retarded		
	The term is related to the following notions: mental ability (examined by tests), phase of development (from birth to 15 years of age), under average (according to tests under 85%), ability of adaptation to the social environment. Students may be characterised as mentally retarded when their mental ability is less than 60%. According to the Presidential Decree 603/82 assessment is made by one medical pedagogical unit (#42) all over the country and regional visiting committees (P.D 472/83), via minimum competency, performance, association (and recently computer-assisted) and individualised tests. The Ministry of Health and Social Affairs administers these units. Students with a mentally handicap are characterised by the units as able to be educated (IQ between 50 & 70), able to be trained (IQ between 30 and 50) and profoundly retarded (under 30). According to the diagnosis, the Ministry of Education classifies the students to the appropriate school unit. Special curricula are offered for for students able to be educated (IQ between 50 and 70) and able to be trained (IQ between 30 and 50).		

Table 3.2. **Allocation of categories of students with disabilities, difficulties, disadvantages included in the resources definition to cross-national categories A, B, C** (*cont.*)

	Cross-national category A	Cross-national category B	Cross-national Category C
Hungary	**1 Educable mental retardation** *Slight cognitive dysfunction based on impairment of the brain. This group belongs to the IQ range 51-70.* **2 Trainable mental retardation** *Severe cognitive dysfunction based on impairment of the brain. This group falls into the IQ range 30-50.* **3 Visual disabilities** *Blindness or low vision based on impairment of the biological visual organs.* **4 Hearing disabilities** *Deafness or hard of hearing based on impairment of the hearing organs.* **5 Motoric disabilities** *Various forms of motor dysfunction based on impairment of organs of movement.* **6 Speech disabilities** *Various forms of speech disorders based on impairment of the speech organs or based on the slow development of language.* **7 Other disabilities** *Various other forms of learning difficulties and/or behavioural problems based on some known or undetected but supposed brain disorder (dyslexia, dysgraphia, autism, etc.).*		**8 (4.1) Children of minorities** **9 (4.2) Disadvantaged pupils/pupils at risk**
Ireland	**1 Visually impaired** *Visually impaired pupils are those who have been formally identified by an ophthalmologist in accordance with agreed criteria.* **2 Hearing impaired** *Hearing impaired pupils are those whose hearing is affected to an extent that renders the understanding of speech through the ear alone, with or without a hearing aid, difficult or impossible.* **3 Mild mental handicap** *Pupils with mild mental handicap have significantly below average general intellectual functioning, associated with*	**5 Emotionally disturbed/behavioural disorders** *This term includes pupils with behavioural and conduct disorders as well as those with emotional disturbance. Emotional and/or behavioural disorder can be defined as an abnormality of behaviour sufficiently marked and prolonged to cause handicap in the pupil and/or serious distress or disturbance in the family, school, or community.*	**10 Children of travelling families** *Children of an identifiable group of people, identified both by themselves and by members of the "settled" community, as people with a distinctive lifestyle, traditionally of a nomadic nature but not now habitual wanderers. They have needs, wants and values different in some ways from those of the settled community.*

Table 3.2. **Allocation of categories of students with disabilities, difficulties, disadvantages included in the resources definition to cross-national categories A, B, C** (*cont.*)

	Cross-national category A	Cross-national category B	Cross-national Category C
Ireland	*impairment in adaptive behaviour. Such pupils would lie within the IQ range 50-70.* **4 Moderate mental handicap** *A pupil with moderate mental handicap falls within the IQ range 35-50, insofar as an intelligence quotient may be used as an indicator of mental disability. Many will have accompanying disabilities.* **7 Physically handicapped** *Pupils with physical handicap have permanent or protracted disabilities arising from conditions such as congenital deformities, spina bifida and/or hydrocephalus, muscular dystrophy, cerebral palsy, brittle bones, haemophilia, cystic fibrosis, asthma, or severe accidental injury.* **8 Specific speech and language disorders** *Pupils with specific speech and language disorders are those whose non-verbal ability is in the average band or higher and whose skill in understanding or expressing themselves through the medium of spoken language is severely impaired.* **9 Specific learning disability** *Specific learning disability is used to describe impairments in specific areas such as reading, writing, spelling and arithmetical notation, the primary cause of which is not attributable to assessed ability being below the average range, to defective sight or hearing, emotional factors, a physical condition or to any extrinsic adverse circumstances.* **11 Severely and profoundly mentally handicapped** *A person with severe mental handicap is described as having an IQ in the range 20-35. A person with profound mental handicap is described as having an IQ under 20. Most will have other disabilities.* **12 Multiply handicapped** *A multiply handicapped pupil has two or more disabilities.*	**6 Severely emotional/behavioural disorder** *As above, to a more serious level.* **15 Pupils in need of remedial teaching** *Pupils in mainstream schools who have clearly observable difficulties in acquiring basic skills in literacy and or numeracy, or who have some difficulties in learning of a more general nature.*	**13 Young offenders** *Children in the age range of 12-16 years who: a) have been convicted of a crime, b) are on remand by the courts, c) are out of control and are under a care order.* **14 Children in schools serving disadvantage areas** *Educationally disadvantaged areas are those where the quality of the educational environment is low in most of the homes, where the level of education attained by the mother is low in most cases and where there are indicators of relative poverty regarding most homes, e.g. living in state housing, having a medical card.* **16 Children of refugees** *Children of parents who have been granted political asylum in Ireland.*

Table 3.2. **Allocation of categories of students with disabilities, difficulties, disadvantages included in the resources definition to cross-national categories A, B, C** *(cont.)*

	Cross-national category A	Cross-national category B	Cross-national Category C
Italy	**1 Visual impairment** *Includes blind children and partially sighted children.* **2 Hearing impairment** *Includes deaf children and partially deaf children.* **3 Moderate mental handicap** *This category includes both mild mental retardation and moderate mental retardation.* *It includes therefore those pupils who are classified as "educable" (that is, that can acquire the knowledge in skills demanded of the final year of primary education - age 10–11) and as "trainable" (that is, that can acquire the knowledge in skills demanded of the second year of primary education - age 7–8).* *The IQ levels of these pupils range from 70 to 35–40.* **4 Severe mental handicap** *This category includes both the group with severe mental retardation and the group with profound mental retardation. It includes pupils who can at most acquire a minimum level of communicative language and pupils who at most can acquire very basic self-care and communication skills.* *The IQ levels of these pupils range from 35–40 to under 20–25.* **5 Mild physical handicap** *Children with a slight motorial impairment and cr a manual impairment, that would not prevent from gaining a relative autonomy.* **6 Severe physical handicap** *Children with a profound motorial impairment ard or a manual impairment, deeply affecting personal autonomy. These children necessitate adequate and continuous assistance.* **7 Multiple handicap** *Children with one or more of the impairments included in categories from 1 to 6. Residual category.*		

OECD 2000

Table 3.2. **Allocation of categories of students with disabilities, difficulties, disadvantages included in the resources definition to cross-national categories A, B, C** (cont.)

	Cross-national category A	Cross-national category B	Cross-national Category C
Korea	**1 Visual impairments** *People who have visual acuity of lower than 0.04 in both eyes with correction. People who can't use vision in learning due to serious visual damages and rely on hearing and touch as main ways of learning. People who have visual acuity of better than 0.04, but have difficulties in performing visual tasks even through specific instructional aids or modification of learning materials. People who can perform visual tasks only by means of specific optical instruments, learning media, or equipments.* **2 Hearing impairments** *People who have a hearing loss greater than 90 dB in both ears. People who can't communicate or have difficulties in communicating with others by vocal language with the use of hearing aids due to serious hearing loss. People who are unable to utilise auditory functions in daily linguistic life and have difficulties in being educated with non-disabled persons.* **3 Mental retardation** *People who score below IQ 75 and have deficits in adaptive behaviours.* **4 Physical impairments** *People who have disabilities in function and shape of body, and have difficulties in learning in general educational facilities, because they have disability or difficulty in sustaining body or movements of hands and feet.* **6 Speech impairments** *People who have disabilities in communicating with others and learning due to articulation disorder, fluency disorder, acoustic disorder, and sign disorder.* **8 Otherwise physical and psychological impairments**	**7 Learning disabilities** *People who have disabilities in learning specific subject areas such as arithmetic, speaking, reading, writing, etc.*	**5 Emotional disturbances (including autism)** *People who have an inability in learning which cannot be explained by intellectual, physical or sensory factors. People who have an inability to build or maintain positive relationships with peers and teachers. People who exhibit inappropriate behaviour or feelings under normal circumstances. People who express a general pervasive mood of unhappiness or depression. People who have a tendency to develop physical symptoms or fears associated with personal or school problems.*
Netherlands	1 Deaf children 2 Hard of hearing 3 Language & communication disabilities 4 Visual handicap 5 Physically handicapped motor impairment 6 Other health impairments (no long hospitalisation) 8 Profound mental handicap, severe learning disabilities	7 Learning disabilities 10 Children with special educational needs/learning disabilities 13 Infant whose development is endangered	14 (4.1) Children from disadvantaged backgrounds 15 (4.2) Children in vocational training with learning difficulties

Table 3.2. **Allocation of categories of students with disabilities, difficulties, disadvantages included in the resources definition to cross-national categories A, B, C** (*cont.*)

	Cross-national category A	Cross-national category B	Cross-national Category C
Netherlands	9 **Deviant behaviour** 11 **Chronic conditions requiring pedological institutes** 12 **Multiply handicapped** NO DEFINITIONS OF CATEGORIES CURRENTLY MADE AVAILABLE		
New Zealand	1 **Deaf or hearing impaired – schools** *Special schools for students who are deaf or hearing impaired.* 2 **Deaf or hearing impaired students – attached units** *Resource teachers of the deaf and hearing impaired, special education attached units for students who are deaf or hearing impaired.* 3 **Blind or visually impaired** *Special schools for students who are blind or who have a visual impairment. Visual resource teachers are resource teacher of visually impaired students.* 6 **Physical disabilities – schools** *Special schools for students with a physical disability.* 7 **Physical disabilities – units and teachers** *Attached special education units for students with physical disability and resource teachers for students with physical disability.* 8 **Intellectual disabilities – schools** *Day special schools for students with intellectual disability.* 9 **Intellectual disabilities – units and teachers** *Special education units for students with an intellectual disability.* 10 **Medical and/or health impairments** *Students in hospitals, psychopaedic hospitals, health camps and attached hospital class teachers.* 14 **Language difficulties** *Units for students with severe language difficulties, including speech – language difficulties.*	4 **Slow learners combined with emotional and behaviour difficulties** 5 **Emotional and/or behaviour difficulties/disorders** 11 **Students with severe social difficulties** *Students in schools which are part of the department of social welfare institutions.* 12 **Behaviour problems** *Students in adjustment classes who have behavioural problems and also any students on the rolls of guidance and learning unit teachers.* 13 **Learning difficulties** *Resource teachers with special needs and attached special education units for students with learning difficulties, including assessment classes, special classes and experience units.*	15 **(4.1) English for speakers of other languages (ESOL)** *This is for students who have the highest English language needs according to assessment criteria in the four modes (listening, speaking, reading and writing).* 16 **(4.2) Truancy** *Truancy is an unjustified absence from school. The Ministry provides funding support to 115 District Truancy Services to support schools in their work on absenteeism and truancy. The Ministry also regards non-enrolment as a form of truancy, and funds the National Non-enrolment Truancy Service (NETS) to deal with it.* 17 **(4.3) Targeted funding for educational achievement** *Targeted Funding for Educational Achievement (TFEA) is intended to assist schools to remedy areas of educational disadvantage which are found in particular communities. The disadvantages envisaged here are those which arise on socio-economic grounds rather than through physical or intellectual impairments.*

Table 3.2. **Allocation of categories of students with disabilities, difficulties, disadvantages included in the resources definition to cross-national categories A, B, C** (*cont.*)

	Cross-national category A	Cross-national category B	Cross-national Category C
Portugal	**1 Mental disability** *Low, under average intellectual development, together with inadaptation/behavioural problems detected during the child's development period and (negatively) affecting the pupil's educational progress. This category does not include pupils with mental disabilities or problems owing to sight, ear or motor handicaps.*		**8 (4.1) Programme of psycho-pedagogical help** *Additional resources are allocated to students with specific learning difficulties for a certain period of time.*
	2 Physical/motor disability *Serious mobility problems, owing to congenital or other diseases or sequent to traumas or infections (negatively) affecting the pupil's educational progress.*		**9 (4.2) Intercultural programme** *Additional resources are allocated to students whose first language is not Portuguese.*
	3 Sight disability *Sight disability/impairment is in cases of sight problems (even after lens correction) affecting the pupil's educational progress. There are three levels for this type of handicap:* - *Blindness – total lack of sight.* - *Residual sight – 0.1 or less, in the visually impaired person's better eye, after lens correction, or 0.1 or more occurring together with a field of vision limitation of 20 or more.* - *Partial sight – 0.1 to 0.3, after lens correction, or higher than 0.3 with field of vision limitation.*		**10 (4.3) Programme of alternative curriculum**
	4 Hearing disability *Hearing disability in cases of total or partial incapacity in processing linguistic information through hearing, with or without sound amplification, permanent or not. Affecting the pupil's educational progress. There are four levels for this disability:* - *Light hearing impairment – loss of 20 to 40 decibels in the child's better ear.* - *Middle hearing impairment – loss of 40 to 70 decibels in the child's better ear.* - *Serious hearing impairment – loss of 70 to 90 decibels in the child's better ear.* - *Deep hearing impairment – loss of more than 90 decibels in the child's better ear.*		
	5 Emotional instability/disturbance *a) Learning difficulties not explainable by intellectual, senso-motor or health reasons.* *b) Difficulties in maintaining interpersonal relationship, both with peers and adults.*		

Table 3.2. **Allocation of categories of students with disabilities, difficulties, disadvantages included in the resources definition to cross-national categories A, B, C** (cont.)

	Cross-national category A	Cross-national category B	Cross-national Category C
Portugal	c) Inadequate behaviour in normal situations. d) Permanent and generalised expression of sadness and depression. e) Evidence of fear associated to personal or school issues. The concept "emotional disturbance" also covers some psychiatric situations like autism, schizophrenia etc. **6 Specific learning difficulties** *In cases of problems in one or more of the basic processes having to do with understanding or using the written or spoken language and causing deficient hearing, thought, speech, reading, writing, maths, calculation, and all aspects of general school learning. Specific learning difficulties refer to pupils over 6 years of age with comprehension problems, minimal brain malfunction, dyslexia, aphasia, etc. Pupils with learning difficulties owing to mental, motor, hearing or sight impairment or to disadvantaged socio-economic and cultural background/environment are excluded. Speech disorders and Multidisability data are included.* **7 Chronic illnesses, serious health problems** *In cases of chronic and/or serious health situations like a congenital heart condition or other cardio/respiratory syndromes, asthma, haemophilia, diabetes, chronic kidney insufficiency, or other diseases affecting the pupil's school performance (absenteeism, slow task performing, attention deficit disorders/ shorter concentration periods, etc.).*		
Spain	**1 Hearing impaired** *Students with partial or complete hearing loss.* **2 Motor impaired** *Motor system alteration due to a deficient osteo-articular, muscular and/or nervous system activity.* **3 Visual impaired** *Significant or complete vision loss.* **4 Mental handicap** *Intellectual performance significantly below average and substantial limitations in adaptive development, revealed before age 18.*	**7 Highly gifted** *Intellectual capability above average, high degree of devotion to tasks and creativity level.* **9 (4.1) Programmes addressed to students in hospitals or with health problems** *Addressed to students who have serious problems of health and need to be in hospitals or to stay at home.*	**8 (4.2) Students with compensatory education needs** *Addressed to students with social or cultural problems which are the cause of a delay in the achievement of knowledge.* **10 (4.3) Programmes addressed to itinerant students** *Addressed to children whose parents are itinerant workers (temporary, circus, fair).*

Table 3.2. **Allocation of categories of students with disabilities, difficulties, disadvantages included in the resources definition to cross-national categories A, B, C** (*cont.*)

	Cross-national category A	Cross-national category B	Cross-national Category C
Spain	5 **Emotional/behavioural problems** *Personality alteration, generally linked with psychosis and autism.* 6 **Multiple impairment** *Two or more concurrent disabilities.*		
Sweden	1 **Special schools for pupils with impaired hearing, vision and physical disabilities** *Deaf and hard of hearing children with sign language as their first language; deaf and hard of hearing, sight impaired and speech or language impaired children with secondary disability.* 2 **Compulsory school for mentally retarded** *Intellectually handicapped children in the age of 7-16 (ISCED 1 and 2 corresponding to "grundskolan'" for other children).* 3 **Upper secondary school for mentally retarded** *School for intellectually handicapped children that have completed "oblija tonsha sarskolan" (ISCED 3 level).*		
Switzerland	9 **Educable mental handicap** 10 **Trainable mental handicap** 11 **Multiply handicapped** 12 **Physical disabilities** 13 **Behaviour disorders** 14 **Deaf or hard of hearing** 15 **Language disability** 16 **Visual handicap** 17 **Chronic conditions/prolonged hospitalisation** 18 **Multiple disabilities** **NO DEFINITIONS OF CATEGORIES CURRENTLY MADE AVAILABLE**	1 **Learning disabilities/introductory classes** 2 **Learning disabilities/special classes** 3 **Learning disabilities/vocationally oriented classes** 4 **Behavioural difficulties** 6 **Physical disabilities** 7 **Sensory & language impairments** 8 **Students who are ill/hospital classes** 19 **Others of the Group "special curriculum"**	5 **Foreign first language**

Table 3.2. **Allocation of categories of students with disabilities, difficulties, disadvantages included in the resources definition to cross-national categories A, B, C** (*cont.*)

	Cross-national category A	Cross-national category B	Cross-national Category C
Turkey	**1 Visually impaired (includes both blind & low vision children)** *Blind: The ones whose visual acuity, even after all possible correction is below 1/10 and who are unable to use their power of vision in their education. Low vision: The ones whose visual acuity, even after all possible correction is between 1/10 and 3/10 and who are unable to use their vision in their education without of the use of special materials and methods.* **2 Hearing impaired** *Deaf: The ones whose loss of hearing, even after all possible correction is above 70 decibels and who are unable to use their power of hearing in their education. Hard of hearing: The ones whose loss of hearing, even after all possible correction is between 25 and 70 decibels and who are only able to use their power of hearing in their education with of the use of hearing aids.* **3 Orthopaedically handicapped** *The ones who are unable to make use of the educational process satisfactorily because of the defects in their skeleton, nervous system, muscles and joints, ever after all possible correction.* **4 Educable mentally handicapped** *Mentally handicapped whose IQ is between 45 and 75 as measured by various intelligence scales.* **5 Trainable mentally handicapped** *Mentally handicapped whose IQ is between 25 and 45 as measured by various intelligence scales.* **6 Speech impairment** *The ones who have impairments in the flow, rhythm and pitch of their speech and in using their voice and articulation effectively.* **8 Chronically ill** *The ones who need special measures to be taken in their education because of the illnesses which require permanent care and medication.*	**7 Gifted and talented** *The ones whose IQ is 130 or above as measured by measured by various intelligence scales (gifted) or whose IQ is 110 or above as measured by various intelligence scales (talented) who show superior talents in the areas such as fine arts and technical areas as compared to their peers.*	
United Kingdom	**Non-categorical system**		

Table 3.2. **Allocation of categories of students with disabilities, difficulties, disadvantages included in the resources definition to cross-national categories A, B, C** (*cont.*)

	Cross-national category A	Cross-national category B	Cross-national Category C
United States	**1 Mental retardation** *Mental retardation means significantly sub average general intellectual functioning existing concurrently with deficits in adaptive behaviour and manifested during the developmental period that adversely affects a child's educational performance (34 Code of Federal Regulations §300.7).* **2 Speech or language impairment** *"Speech or language impairment" means a communication disorder such as stuttering, impaired articulation, a language impairment, or a voice impairment that adversely affects a child's educational performance (34 code of Federal Regulations §300.7).* **3 Visual impairments** *Visual impairment including blindness means an impairment in vision that, even with correction, adversely affects a child's educational performance. The term includes both partial sight and blindness. 534 Code of Federal Regulations §300.7).* **5 Orthopedic impairments** *Orthopedic impairment means a severe orthopedic impairment that adversely affects a child's educational performance. The term includes impairments caused by congenital anomaly (e.g. clubfoot, absence of some member, etc.), impairments caused by disease (e.g. poliomyelitis, bone tuberculosis, etc.), and impairments from other causes (e.g. cerebral palsy, amputations, and fractures or burns that cause contractors) (34 Code of Federal Regulations §300.7).* **6 Other health impairments** *Other health impairment means having limited strength, vitality or alertness, due to chronic or acute health problems such as a heart condition, tuberculosis, rheumatic fever, nephritis, asthma, sickle cell anaemia, haemophilia, epilepsy, lead poisoning, leukaemia, or diabetes that adversely affects a child's educational performance (34 Code of Federal Regulations §300.7).* **8 Deaf/Blindness** *Deaf-Blindness means concomitant hearing and visual impairments, the combination of which causes such severe*	**4 Emotional disturbance** *Emotional disturbance is defined as follows:* *i) the term means a condition exhibiting one or more of the following characteristics over a long period of time and to a marked degree that adversely affects a child's educational performance: a) an inability to learn that cannot be explained by intellectual, sensory, or health factors; b) an inability to build or maintain satisfactory interpersonal relationships with peers and teachers; c) inappropriate types of behaviour or feelings under normal circumstances; d) a general pervasive mood of unhappiness or depression; or e) a tendency to develop physical symptoms or fears associated with personal or school problems.* *ii) The term does not apply to children who are socially maladjusted, unless it is determined that they have a serious emotional disturbance (34 Code of Federal Regulations §300.7).* **7 Specific learning disability** *Specific learning disability means a disorder in one or more of the basic psychological processes involved in understanding or in using language, spoken or written, that may manifest itself in an imperfect ability to listen, think, speak, read, write, spell, or to do mathematical calculations. The term includes such conditions as perceptual disabilities, brain injury, minimal brain dysfunction, dyslexia, and developmental aphasia. The term does not apply to children who have learning problems that are primarily the result of visual, hearing, or motor disabilities, of mental retardation, of emotional disturbance, or of environmental, cultural, or economic disadvantage (34 code of federal regulations §300.7).*	**13 (4.1) Title 1 – Disadvantaged students**

Table 3.2. **Allocation of categories of students with disabilities, difficulties, disadvantages included in the resources definition to cross-national categories A, B, C** (*cont.*)

	Cross-national category A	Cross-national category B	Cross-national Category C
United States	communication and other developmental and educational problems that they cannot be accommodated in special education programmes solely for children with deafness or children with blindness (34 Code of Federal Regulations §300.7).		
	9 Multiple disabilities Multiple disabilities means concomitant impairments (such as mental retardation-blindness, mental retardation-orthopaedic impairment, etc.), the combination of which causes such severe educational problems they cannot be accommodated in special education programmes solely for one of the impairments. The term does not include deaf-blindness (34 Code of Federal Regulations §300.7).		
	10 Hearing impairments Hearing impairment includes deafness and hard of hearing. Deafness means a hearing impairment that is so severe that the child is impaired in processing linguistic information through hearing, with or without amplification, that adversely affects a child's educational performance. Hard of hearing means an impairment in hearing, whether permanent or fluctuation, that adversely affects a child's educational performance but that is not included under the definition of deafness in this section (34 Code of Federal Regulation §300.7).		
	11 Autism Autism means a developmental disability significantly affecting verbal and no verbal communication and social interaction, generally evident before age 3, that adversely affects a child's educational performance. Other characteristics often associated with autism are engagement in repetitive activities and stereotyped movements, resistance to environmental change or change in daily routines, and unusual responses to sensory experiences. The term does not apply if a child's educational performance's adversely affected primarily because the child has a serious emotional disturbance, as defined in paragraph (b) (9) of this section (see description of emotional disturbance given in Category 4 above [34 Code of Federal Regulations §300.7].		

OECD 2000

Table 3.2. **Allocation of categories of students with disabilities, difficulties, disadvantages included in the resources definition to cross-national categories A, B, C** (*cont.*)

	Cross-national category A	Cross-national category B	Cross-national Category C
United States	**12 Traumatic brain injury** *Traumatic brain injury means an acquired injury to the brain caused by an external physical force, resulting in total or partial functional disability or psychosocial impairment, or both, that adversely affects a child's educational performance. The term applies to open or closed head injuries resulting in impairments in one or more areas, such as cognition; language; memory; attention; reasoning; abstract thinking; judgement; problem-solving; sensory; perceptual and motor abilities; psychosocial behaviour; physical functions; information processing; and speech. The term does not apply to brain injuries that are congenital or degenerative, or brain injuries induced by birth trauma (34 Code of Federal Regulations §300.7).*		

Note: (4.1), (4.2), etc., shows those categories which receive additional resources but which are not part of national categories of special educational needs.

Austria. Standardised definitions of the various kinds of disabilities/impairments have not been provided for special needs sducation. Since integration in primary schools has been implemented by law in 1993 the definition of special educational needs includes all children, who, referring to their physical or psychological impairment, cannot follow the curriculum of the regular school without receiving additional special support. In order to classify the nature and the degree of the child's disability and to provide specific measures and resources a formal procedure (Statement of SEN) is carried out by the local school board. This statement is based on the responsible teacher's assessment which, in case of need. may be supplemented by psychological, medical or therapeutic expertise.

Chapter 4

COMPARATIVE ANALYSIS OF QUANTITATIVE DATA BASED ON NATIONAL CATEGORIES OF DISABILITIES

Background

This chapter analyses the data provided by countries by the national categories of disability that each country uses based on the returns given in Tables 2, 3 and 4 of the instrument (see Annex 3). An additional factor is that only students placed by countries into cross-national categories A and B are used, since these two categories cover all those students who may have an identifiable biological impairment associated with their learning difficulties. The data also cover only those students who are registered by the education authorities and they suffer from the limitation of not including disabled students of the relevant age who are outside of the education system. However, earlier work (OECD, 1995) showed that these numbers would be either very small or non-existent since many countries have 100% of students of school age under the aegis of the education authorities.

The data are broken down by disability categories and presented as proportions of the total numbers of students in primary and lower secondary education. In addition, information is provided on the place or location of these students' education *i.e.* in regular classes, special classes or special schools, expressed as proportions of the total numbers of students in that disability category in the particular location.

The data in this chapter have been assembled in the full knowledge of the difficulty of making international comparisons on the basis of national categories of disability. However, it was considered useful to carry out this analysis in order to keep touch with the basic data in the form in which it was presented, using terminology that many readers would more readily follow and to provide the context for comparisons made through cross-national categories A, B and C. The method used is outlined below. Table 3.2 provides the background information showing why such comparisons are hazardous. First not all countries use categorical models, second the disability categories used are not uniform across countries, and third the definitions of the categories, when available, vary among countries. It is of course partly for these reasons that the resources model and the cross-national categorisation system are being developed.

Methodology

In order to make comparisons between countries based on national categories of disability a number of simplifying assumptions must be made which will bring similar students together within a common descriptive categorical name. For a number of categories this is relatively straightforward. It applies for the most part to the categories of blind and partially sighted, deaf and partially hearing, emotional and behaviour difficulties, physical disabilities, multiple disabilities, speech and language disabilities, and those who are hospitalised.

For the remaining categories, namely: severe learning difficulties, moderate learning difficulties, light learning difficulties, learning disabilities, and autism there are problems of substantial variation in the descriptions of students so placed. The OECD Secretariat allotted students falling under the various national

53

descriptions which cover these students with learning difficulties into the four categories of W-LD, X-LD Y-LD Z-LD which provide a rank order of degree of learning difficulty/disability from greatest to least. In approximate terms W-LD refers to those students with IQs in the range 0-40/50; X-LD 40/50-70; Y-LD 70-85; and Z-LD 85+.

Such a procedure is not without its problems however. For instance, if a country is not included in the table on severe learning difficulties, this does not mean that there are no such children with learning difficulties at this level or that there is no provision. It is much more likely that these children are included in another category. In the United States for example, students displaying severe and moderate learning difficulties are included under the general heading of "mental retardation". For those countries included in these comparisons, Table 4.2 supplies the analysis through which national categories have been placed into four collective categories of learning difficulties plus emotional and behavioural difficulties and multiple disabilities.

Further analysis reported at the end of the chapter is made of the data provided on the proportions of students in these various categories. This approach attempts to make allowance for the differing definitions pertaining to students in these categories.

It is worth pointing out again that these problems present formidable challenges for international comparisons and is one of the reasons for adopting a resources-based model as well as the cross-national categories of A, B and C as described in earlier chapters.

Data on individual categories of disability

Chart 4.1 (A to L) shows the percentages of students in the 12 main categories of disability used by participating countries. The percentages are calculated by dividing the number of students in each category by the total number of students in primary and lower secondary education (ISCED 1 and 2), with the exception of Belgium (Flemish Community) which includes upper secondary students (ISCED 3) and Turkey which only includes primary education students (ISCED 1).

The figures are based on full-time study. Data refer to the school year 1995/96 with the exception of Finland where the data cover 1994/95, France 1994 to 1998, and Belgium (Flemish Community), Italy, the Netherlands, Spain and Switzerland where data cover 1996/97. The figures are based on both public and private institutions, unless otherwise indicated.

The charts are ranked in ascending order of magnitude according to the proportions of students registered. Charts 4.1A-4.1L are based on the proportions of students in individual disability categories as a percentage of all students in primary and lower secondary education. In Charts 4.2-4.13 the country data are placed in ascending order according to the proportions of students educated in special schools.

From the point of view of making international comparisons, Chart 4.1 reveals two major issues. First, comparison is hampered by the inconsistent use of categories among countries. Only four, the blind and partially sighted (4.1A), the deaf and partially hearing (4.1B), emotional and behavioural difficulties (4.1C) and those with physical disabilities (4.1D) are used by the majority of countries. The remaining eight are used to varying degrees. All 12 categories are discussed in greater detail in the following sections. Second, close inspection of the individual categories reveals unexpectedly large differences among countries in the proportions of students identified. The information needed to understand these differences is simply not readily available.

Also note that there is a significant amount of double counting when the numbers of pupils in regular classes are added together in Ireland, *e.g.* it is estimated that some 19 000 pupils are included in more than one category. This has been taken into account here and adjustments made. Nonetheless, proportions may be underestimated because of some missing data in lower secondary education.

Chart 4.1. **Percentage of pupils in primary and lower secondary education by disability category and by country**

NB : Only includes data which can be readily placed in one of the 12 categories below

A. Blind and Partially Sighted

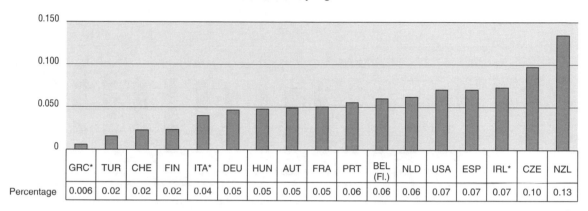

	GRC*	TUR	CHE	FIN	ITA*	DEU	HUN	AUT	FRA	PRT	BEL (Fl.)	NLD	USA	ESP	IRL*	CZE	NZL
Percentage	0.006	0.02	0.02	0.02	0.04	0.05	0.05	0.05	0.05	0.06	0.06	0.06	0.07	0.07	0.07	0.10	0.13

B. Deaf and Partially Hearing

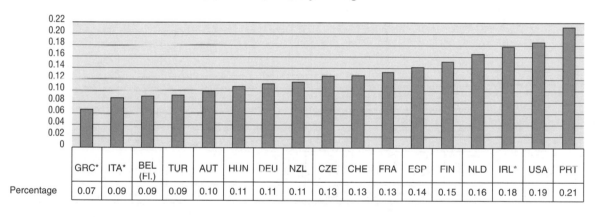

	GRC*	ITA*	BEL (Fl.)	TUR	AUT	HUN	DEU	NZL	CZE	CHE	FRA	ESP	FIN	NLD	IRL*	USA	PRT
Percentage	0.07	0.09	0.09	0.09	0.10	0.11	0.11	0.11	0.13	0.13	0.13	0.14	0.15	0.16	0.18	0.19	0.21

C. Emotional and Behavioural Difficulties

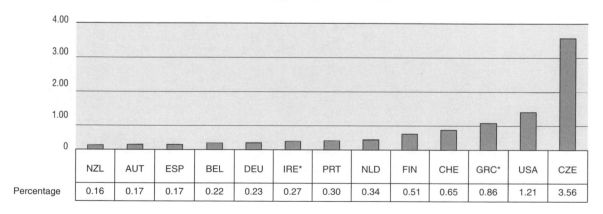

	NZL	AUT	ESP	BEL	DEU	IRE*	PRT	NLD	FIN	CHE	GRC*	USA	CZE
Percentage	0.16	0.17	0.17	0.22	0.23	0.27	0.30	0.34	0.51	0.65	0.86	1.21	3.56

* Public institutions only.

Chart 4.1. **Percentage of pupils in primary and lower secondary education by disability category and by country** *(cont.)*

NB : Only includes data which can be readily placed in one of the 12 categories below

D. Physical Disability

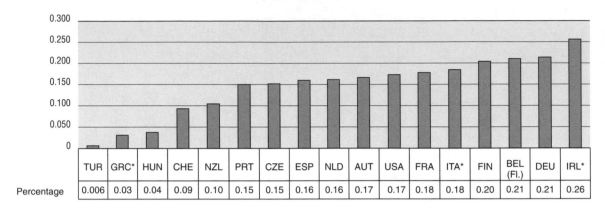

	TUR	GRC*	HUN	CHE	NZL	PRT	CZE	ESP	NLD	AUT	USA	FRA	ITA*	FIN	BEL (Fl.)	DEU	IRL*
Percentage	0.006	0.03	0.04	0.09	0.10	0.15	0.15	0.16	0.16	0.17	0.17	0.18	0.18	0.20	0.21	0.21	0.26

E. Speech and Language Difficulties

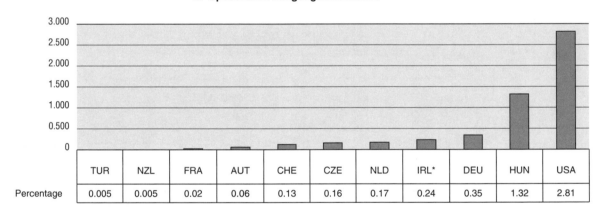

	TUR	NZL	FRA	AUT	CHE	CZE	NLD	IRL*	DEU	HUN	USA
Percentage	0.005	0.005	0.02	0.06	0.13	0.16	0.17	0.24	0.35	1.32	2.81

F. Hospital

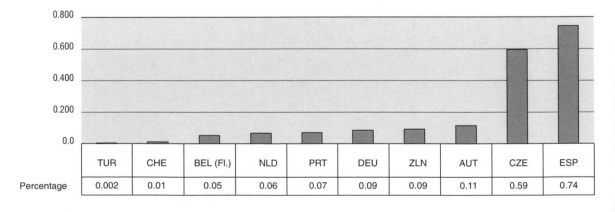

	TUR	CHE	BEL (Fl.)	NLD	PRT	DEU	ZLN	AUT	CZE	ESP
Percentage	0.002	0.01	0.05	0.06	0.07	0.09	0.09	0.11	0.59	0.74

* Public institutions only.

Chart 4.1. **Percentage of pupils in primary and lower secondary education by disability category and by country** *(cont.)*

NB : Only includes data which can be readily placed in one of the 12 categories below

G. Multiple Disabilities

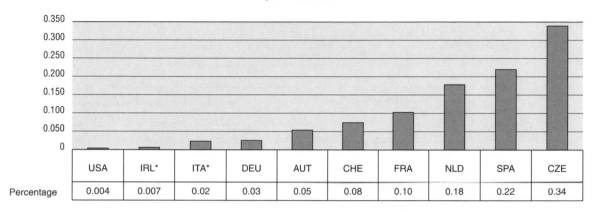

	USA	IRL*	ITA*	DEU	AUT	CHE	FRA	NLD	SPA	CZE
Percentage	0.004	0.007	0.02	0.03	0.05	0.08	0.10	0.18	0.22	0.34

H. Autistic

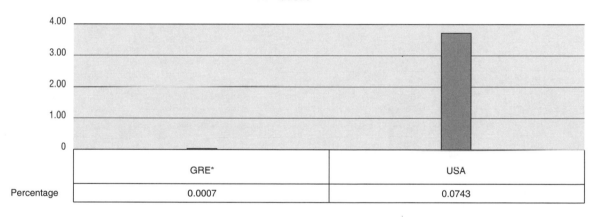

	GRE*	USA
Percentage	0.0007	0.0743

I. Severe Learning Difficulties

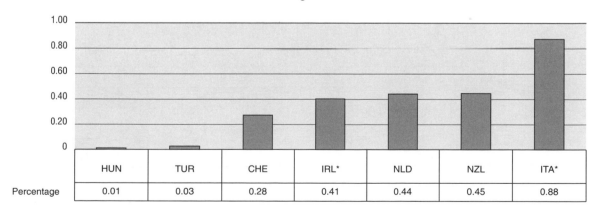

	HUN	TUR	CHE	IRL*	NLD	NZL	ITA*
Percentage	0.01	0.03	0.28	0.41	0.44	0.45	0.88

* Public institutions only.

OECD 2000

Chart 4.1. **Percentage of pupils in primary and lower secondary education by disability category and by country** *(cont.)*

NB : Only includes data which can be readily placed in one of the 12 categories below

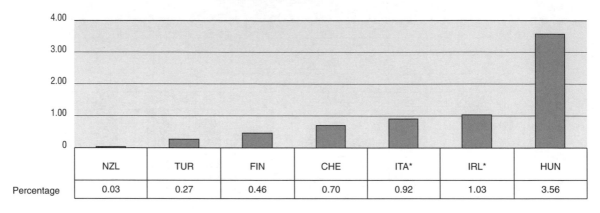

J. Moderate Learning Difficulties

	NZL	TUR	FIN	CHE	ITA*	IRL*	HUN
Percentage	0.03	0.27	0.46	0.70	0.92	1.03	3.56

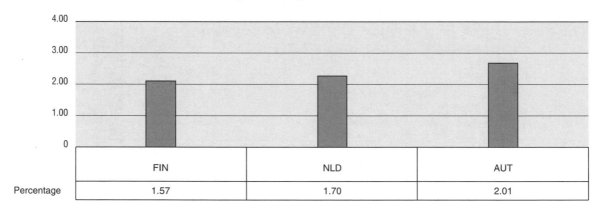

K. Light Learning Difficulties

	FIN	NLD	AUT
Percentage	1.57	1.70	2.01

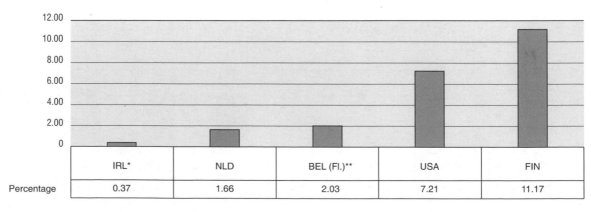

L. Learning Disabilities

	IRL*	NLD	BEL (Fl.)**	USA	FIN
Percentage	0.37	1.66	2.03	7.21	11.17

*Public institutions only.
**Belgium (Flemish Community): primary education only.

Description by category

Blind and partially sighted

The statistics on the categories covering blind and partially sighted students are treated separately in only a few countries (Austria, France, and Germany) but in most are brought together as a single category which is used for reporting the data here.

As can be seen from Chart 4.1A the proportion of blind and partially sighted students varies substantially from country to country. The lowest percentage being in Greece (0.006%) and the highest in New Zealand (0.13%). This means that some countries register in their education statistics 21.7 times as many as others. Even if the highest and lowest figures are ignored the differences remain substantial with the Czech Republic (0.10%), registering five times as many as France, Switzerland and Turkey (0.02%).

Chart 4.2 shows that four countries use regular classes, special classes and special schools; the Czech Republic (35.70%, 1.99%, 62.31%), France (22.45%, 17.47%, 60.08%), Turkey (42.59%, 2.90%, 54.50%), and the United States (68.32%, 17.07%, 14.61%).

Nine countries have a binary system dividing these students between regular classes and special schools, Austria (32.09% estimated, 67.91%), the Flemish Community of Belgium (31.35%, 68.65%), Finland (61.31%, 38.69%), Ireland (78.07%, 21.93%), Italy (95.99%, 4.01%), the Netherlands (49.59% estimated, 50.41%), New Zealand (88.62%, 11.38%), Portugal (95.97%, 4.03%), and Spain (76.20%, 23.80%). In Greece, pupils are located in special classes (18.18%) and in special schools (81.82%). In Germany and Switzerland the majority of students are educated in special schools but missing data prevent the calculation of the proportions in each location.

At the extremes, the location of education varies considerably. In Italy and Portugal 96% are educated in regular schools and this may be contrasted with those in the countries identified above where over two thirds are educated in special schools.

Chart 4.2. **Proportion of blind and partially sighted pupils in primary and lower secondary education by location and by country**

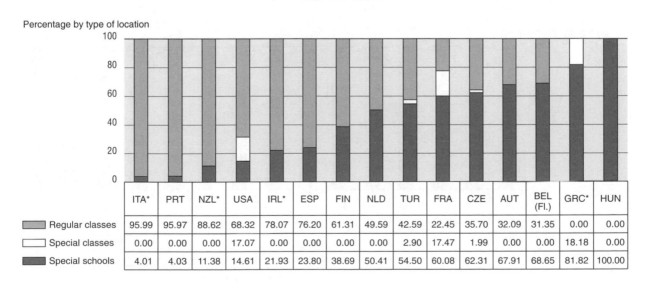

Percentage by type of location

	ITA*	PRT	NZL*	USA	IRL*	ESP	FIN	NLD	TUR	FRA	CZE	AUT	BEL (Fl.)	GRC*	HUN
Regular classes	95.99	95.97	88.62	68.32	78.07	76.20	61.31	49.59	42.59	22.45	35.70	32.09	31.35	0.00	0.00
Special classes	0.00	0.00	0.00	17.07	0.00	0.00	0.00	0.00	2.90	17.47	1.99	0.00	0.00	18.18	0.00
Special schools	4.01	4.03	11.38	14.61	21.93	23.80	38.69	50.41	54.50	60.08	62.31	67.91	68.65	81.82	100.00

* Public institutions only.
Austria, Netherlands: figures for regular classes are estimates.
Belgium (Flemish Community): the figures for pupils with special educational needs in regular classes are underestimated because of the method used to distribute resources.
Italy: special schools are public and private.
New Zealand: special schools are government dependent private institutions.

Deaf and partially hearing

As for blind and partially sighted students, the statistics gathered on categories covering deaf and partially hearing pupils are treated separately in only a few countries (Austria, France, Germany, and the Netherlands). In most countries, they are treated as a single entity and this method is adopted here.

As can be seen from Chart 4.1B the proportion of deaf and partially hearing students registered in educational statistics varies substantially from country to country. The lowest percentage being Greece 0.07% and the highest 0.21% in Portugal. This means that some countries register three times as many as others. Even if the highest and lowest are ignored the differences remain, with the United States (0.19%) registering almost 2.1 times as many as Belgium (Flemish Community), Italy or Turkey (0.09%).

Chart 4.3 reveals that nine countries divide deaf and partially hearing pupils among regular classes, special classes and special schools, the Czech Republic (23.52%, 0.15% 76.33%), Finland (4.50%, 10.91% 84.59%), France (19.43%, 16.16%, 64.41%), Ireland (56.19%, 5.35%, 38.45%), Italy (95.04%, 1.04%, 3.92%), New Zealand (59.62%, 11.76%, 28.62%), Portugal (55.74%, 37.67%, 6.59%), Turkey (12.31%, 8.26%, 79.43%) and the United States (55.04%, 26.76%, 18.20%).

Five countries have a binary system. Regular classes and special schools are used in Austria (32.27% estimated, 67.73%), the Flemish Community of Belgium (26.84%, 73.16%), the Netherlands (31.41% estimated, 68.59%), Spain (79.33%, 20.67%). In Greece, they attend either special classes (42.90%) or special schools (57.10%). In Hungary they are all educated in special schools. In Germany and Switzerland the majority of students are educated in special schools but missing data prevent the calculation of the proportions in each location.

At the extremes the location of education varies considerably with the majority being educated in regular classes in Italy in contrast to Hungary where none or very few are registered in regular schools.

Chart 4.3. **Proportion of deaf and partially hearing pupils in primary and lower secondary education by location and by country**

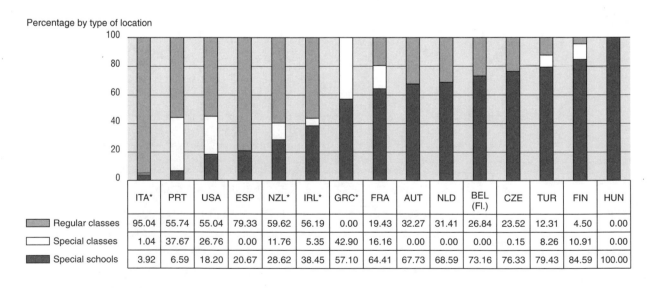

Percentage by type of location

	ITA*	PRT	USA	ESP	NZL*	IRL*	GRC*	FRA	AUT	NLD	BEL (Fl.)	CZE	TUR	FIN	HUN
Regular classes	95.04	55.74	55.04	79.33	59.62	56.19	0.00	19.43	32.27	31.41	26.84	23.52	12.31	4.50	0.00
Special classes	1.04	37.67	26.76	0.00	11.76	5.35	42.90	16.16	0.00	0.00	0.00	0.15	8.26	10.91	0.00
Special schools	3.92	6.59	18.20	20.67	28.62	38.45	57.10	64.41	67.73	68.59	73.16	76.33	79.43	84.59	100.00

* Public institutions only.
Austria, Netherlands: figures for regular classes are estimates.
Belgium (Flemish Community): the figures for pupils with special educational needs in regular classes are underestimated because of the method used to distribute resources.
Italy: special schools are public and private.

Emotional and behavioural difficulties

It is of interest to note that given the apparent rise in the numbers of students described as having behaviour difficulties, not all countries use such a category. For those who do, there is evidence for a greater differentiation in terms of location than in the two preceding clusters of categories.

As can be seen from Chart 4.1C the proportion of students with emotional and behavioural difficulties varies substantially from country to country. The lowest percentage being in New Zealand (0.16%) and the highest in the Czech Republic (3.56%). This means that some countries register in educational statistics 22.3 times as many as others. However, if the two most extreme countries are ignored this figure is substantially reduced to 7.1 (United States 1.21%, and Spain or Austria 0.17%).

Chart 4.4 shows that five countries use regular classes, special classes and special schools. Austria (31.92% estimated, 0.46%, 67.62%), Czech Republic (70.58%, 26.13%, 3.29%) Finland (3.32%, 79.80%, 16.88%), New Zealand (85.17%, 4.48%, 10.34%) and the United States (47.13%, 34.30%, 18.57%).

Five countries use two locations. Regular classes and special schools are used in the Flemish Community of Belgium (2.11%, 97.89%), Ireland (68.87%, 31.13%), the Netherlands (4.85% estimated, 95.15%) and Spain (60.94%, 39.06%). Special classes and special schools are used in Switzerland (64.80%, 35.20%). In Germany the majority of these students are educated in special schools but missing data prevent the calculation of the proportions in each location.

Two countries use only one location. In Greece they are all in special classes, while in Portugal they are all in regular classes.

At the extremes, the location of education varies considerably. In Portugal all children in this category are educated in regular classes which may be contrasted with those countries identified where all or most children are educated in special schools.

Chart 4.4. **Proportion of pupils with emotional and/or behavioural difficulties in primary and lower secondary education by location and by country**

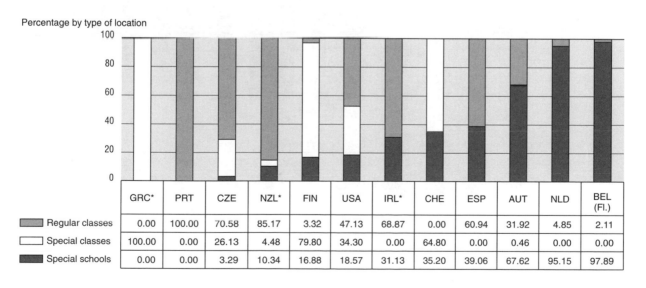

Percentage by type of location

	GRC*	PRT	CZE	NZL*	FIN	USA	IRL*	CHE	ESP	AUT	NLD	BEL (Fl.)
Regular classes	0.00	100.00	70.58	85.17	3.32	47.13	68.87	0.00	60.94	31.92	4.85	2.11
Special classes	100.00	0.00	26.13	4.48	79.80	34.30	0.00	64.80	0.00	0.46	0.00	0.00
Special schools	0.00	0.00	3.29	10.34	16.88	18.57	31.13	35.20	39.06	67.62	95.15	97.89

* Public institutions only.
Austria, Netherlands: figures for regular classes are estimates.
Belgium (Flemish Community): the figures for pupils with special educational needs in regular classes are underestimated because of the method used to distribute resources.
New Zealand: regular classes government dependent private institutions.

OECD 2000

Physical disability

It is readily observable from Chart 4.1D that there is great variation in the proportion of students registered with physical disabilities in all countries. Ireland (0.26%), Germany (0.21%) and the Flemish Community of Belgium (0.21%) have the highest percentages, while the lowest are in Turkey (0.006%), Greece (0.03%), and Hungary (0.04%) which means that Ireland therefore registers in educational statistics 43.3 times as many students as Turkey. Even if the most extreme countries are not considered, Germany and the Flemish Community of Belgium (0.21%) register seven times more than Greece (0.03%).

As shown in Chart 4.5, eight countries use all three locations, regular classes, special classes and special schools; Austria (32.24% estimated, 0.31%, 67.45%), the Czech Republic (53.28%, 0.85%, 45.87%) Finland (5.77%, 37.63%, 56.61%), France (28.68%, 10.57%, 60.74%), Ireland (62.35%, 0.41%, 37.23%), Italy (99.06%, 0.04%, 0.90%), New Zealand (25.17%, 64.34%, 10.49%) and United States (61.54%, 30.50%, 7.96%).

Five countries have systems which distribute these students between regular classes and special schools; the Flemish Community of Belgium (11.77%, 88.23), the Netherlands (33.77% estimated, 66.23%) Portugal (88.17%, 11.83%), Spain (91.25%, 8.75%), and Turkey (77.50%, 22.50%). Three countries use special classes and special schools: Greece (11.35%, 88.65%), Hungary (8.15%, 91.85%) and Switzerland (6.78%, 93.22%) although as may be seen, the majority of students remain in special schools. In Germany the majority of these students are educated in special schools but missing data prevent the calculation of the proportions in each location.

At the extremes the location of education varies considerably. In Italy 99.06% are educated in regular classes in contrast to Switzerland where the majority are in special schools.

Chart 4.5. **Proportion of students with physical disabilities in primary and lower secondary education by location and by country**

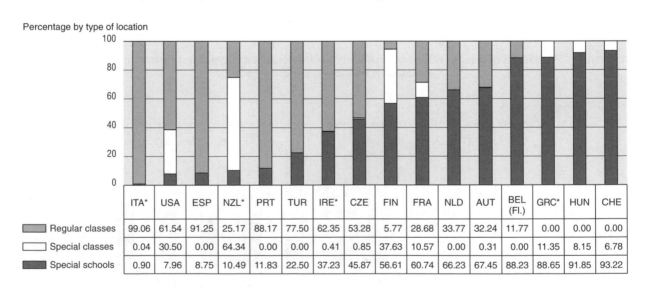

Percentage by type of location

	ITA*	USA	ESP	NZL*	PRT	TUR	IRE*	CZE	FIN	FRA	NLD	AUT	BEL (Fl.)	GRC*	HUN	CHE
Regular classes	99.06	61.54	91.25	25.17	88.17	77.50	62.35	53.28	5.77	28.68	33.77	32.24	11.77	0.00	0.00	0.00
Special classes	0.04	30.50	0.00	64.34	0.00	0.00	0.41	0.85	37.63	10.57	0.00	0.31	0.00	11.35	8.15	6.78
Special schools	0.90	7.96	8.75	10.49	11.83	22.50	37.23	45.87	56.61	60.74	66.23	67.45	88.23	88.65	91.85	93.22

* Public institutions only.
Belgium (Flemish Community): the figures for pupils with special educational needs in regular classes are underestimated because of the method used to distribute resources.
Italy: special schools are public and private.
Netherlands: figures for regular classes are estimates.

Speech and language difficulties

As can be seen from Chart 4.1E the percentages of students registered with speech and language difficulties also vary substantially from country to country. The lowest percentage being in New Zealand (0.005%) and Turkey

(0.005%), and the highest in the United States (2.81%). This means that some countries register 562 times as many as others. However if the extremes are ignored, the variation is considerably reduced with Germany (0.35%) registering 17.5 times more than France (0.02%).

Chart 4.6 reveals that three countries use regular classes, special classes and special schools; the Czech Republic (37.13%, 6.17%, 56.71%), Hungary (95.45%, 2.03%, 2.52%) and the United States (95.08%, 4.50%, 0.42%).

Five countries use only two locations. Special classes and special schools are used in France (3.36%, 96.64%) and Switzerland (22.54%, 77.46%). Regular classes and special schools are used by Austria (32.04% estimated, 67.96%) and the Netherlands (29.43% estimated, 70.57%). Regular classes and special classes are used by Ireland (85.27%, 14.73%). In Germany and Switzerland the majority of these students are educated in special schools but missing data prevent the calculation of the proportions in each location.

In New Zealand all students are in special classes and in Turkey they are all in regular classes.

Thus, at the extremes there is wide variation in the location of education, with some countries using mainly regular classes and others mainly special schools.

Chart 4.6. **Proportion of students with speech and language difficulties in primary and lower secondary education by location and by country**

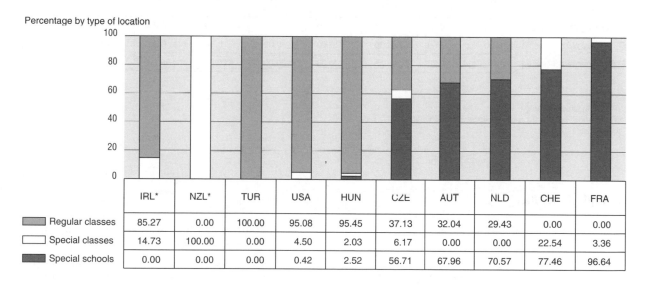

Percentage by type of location

	IRL*	NZL*	TUR	USA	HUN	CZE	AUT	NLD	CHE	FRA
Regular classes	85.27	0.00	100.00	95.08	95.45	37.13	32.04	29.43	0.00	0.00
Special classes	14.73	100.00	0.00	4.50	2.03	6.17	0.00	0.00	22.54	3.36
Special schools	0.00	0.00	0.00	0.42	2.52	56.71	67.96	70.57	77.46	96.64

* Public institutions only.
Austria, Netherlands: figures for regular classes are estimates.
United States: category also covered by severe learning difficulties and moderate learning difficulties.
Note: in Switzerland the category of students with speech and language difficulties is the aggregation of a category grouping language disability and sensory and language impairments.

Hospital

As can be seen from Chart 4.1F, the percentage of students registered as receiving education while hospitalised varies substantially from country to country. The lowest percentage being in Turkey (0.002%) and the highest in Spain (0.74%). This means that some countries register 370 times as many as others. However if the extremes are ignored the differences are considerably reduced, with Austria (0.11%), registering 11 times as many as Switzerland (0.01%).

Chart 4.7 shows that with the exception of the Netherlands which places these students in regular classes (3.17% estimated) and special schools (96.83%), all other countries use one location only, either special schools or regular schools. In Portugal and Spain, those students identified who are located in regular classes are those who need only periodic hospitalisation. The data thus confirm the wide variety of provision which is utilised for these students. In Belgium (Flemish Community), students are in the so-called "hospital schools" for a limited period of time; in the meantime they remain also registered in their regular school.

Chart 4.7. **Proportion of students in hospital in primary and lower secondary education by location and by country**

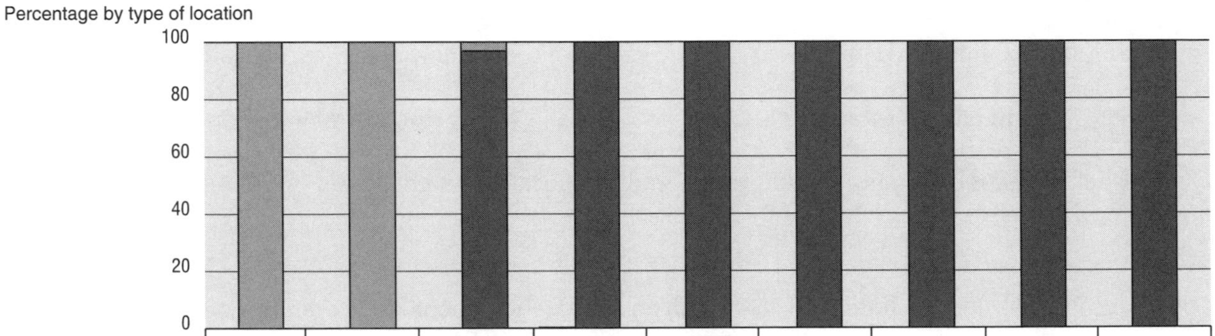

Percentage by type of location

	PRT	ESP	NLD	AUT	BEL (Fl.)	CHE	CZE	NZL*	TUR
Regular classes	100.00	100.00	3.17	0.00	0.00	0.00	0.00	0.00	0.00
Special classes	0.00	0.00	0.00	0.00	0.00	0.00	0.00	0.00	0.00
Special schools	0.00	0.00	96.83	100.00	100.00	100.00	100.00	100.00	100.00

* Public institutions only.
Netherlands: figures for regular classes are estimates.

Multiple disabilities

Ten countries have a category for students with multiple disabilities as Chart 4.1G shows, and again the proportions of students in this category vary substantially from country to country. The lowest percentages are found in the United States (0.004%) and the highest in the Czech Republic (0.34%). This means that some countries register in educational statistics 85 times as many as others do. Even if the extremes are ignored, the differences remain substantial, with Spain (0.22%) registering 31.4 times more than Ireland (0.007%).

Chart 4.8 shows that four countries have systems which use regular classes, special classes and special schools; Austria (32.29% estimated, 4.58%, 63.13%), the Czech Republic (26.49%, 3.31%, 70.20%), Ireland (44.00%, 14.00%, 42.00%) and the United States (20.69%, 40.23%, 39.07%).

Three countries use only two locations, regular schools and special schools; the Netherlands (6.93% estimated, 93.07%) Spain (42.13%, 57.87%). Italy uses special classes (10.82%) and special schools (89.18%). France places all of these students into special schools. In Germany and Switzerland the majority of these students are educated in special schools but missing data prevent the calculation of the proportions in each location.

Provision for these very impaired students appears less varied than for other categories, with most countries using special classes or special schools to educate the majority of these students.

Chart 4.8. **Proportion of students with multiple disabilities in primary and lower secondary education by location and by country**

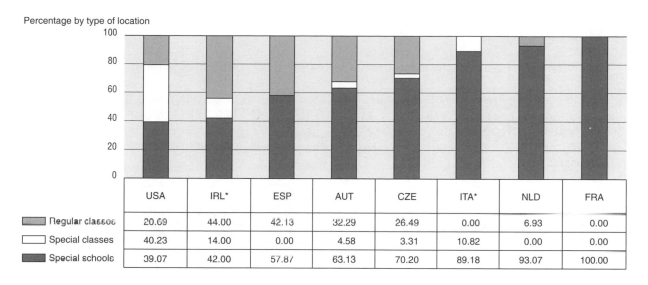

Percentage by type of location

	USA	IRL*	ESP	AUT	CZE	ITA*	NLD	FRA
Regular classes	20.69	44.00	42.13	32.29	26.49	0.00	6.93	0.00
Special classes	40.23	14.00	0.00	4.58	3.31	10.82	0.00	0.00
Special schools	39.07	42.00	57.87	63.13	70.20	89.18	93.07	100.00

* Public institutions only.
Austria, Netherlands: figures for regular classes are estimates.
Ireland: estimated figures.
Italy: special schools are public and private.
Note: In Italy in regular classes the proportion of students with multiple disabilities is not a true zero since they are registered according to the most severe disability.

Autistic

Although there is great interest world wide in the topic of autism only two countries, Greece and the United States, use this category to gather statistics and Chart 4.III shows the variation between them. The United States (0.07%) register 100 times as many as Greece (0.0007%).

Chart 4.9. **Proportion of autistic students in primary and lower secondary education by location and by country**

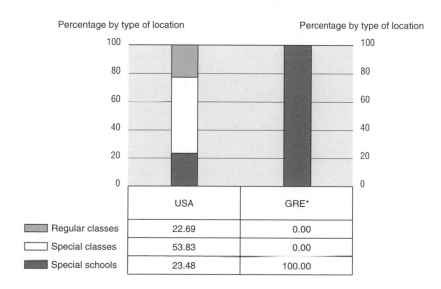

Percentage by type of location

	USA	GRE*
Regular classes	22.69	0.00
Special classes	53.83	0.00
Special schools	23.48	100.00

Chart 4.9 shows that in the United States autistic students are divided among regular classes (22.69%), special classes (53.83%) and special schools (23.48%). In Greece, on the other hand, all autistic students are educated in special schools.

Severe learning difficulties

Seven countries keep statistics for students with severe learning difficulties as Chart 4.11 shows.

As can be seen from Chart 4.11 the proportion of students registered with severe learning difficulties varies substantially from country to country. The lowest percentage being in Hungary (0.01%) and the highest in Italy (0.88%). This means that some countries register 87 times as many as others. Even if the extremes are ignored, the differences remain substantial with New Zealand (0.45%) registering 15 times more than Turkey (0.03%).

Chart 4.10 shows that four countries use regular schools, special classes and special schools; Ireland (4.74%, 4.00%, 91.26%), Italy (98.75%, 0.06%, 1.19%), New Zealand (12.84%, 34.69%, 52.47%), and Turkey (1.43%, 1.37%, 97.21%). The Netherlands uses regular classes (0.09% estimated) and special schools (99.91%) while Hungary places all of these students in special classes. In Switzerland the vast majority of those students are educated in special schools but missing data disallows the calculation of the proportions in each location

At the extremes the location of education varies considerably with almost all of these students being educated in regular classes in Italy in contrast to other countries where the majority are in special schools.

Chart 4.10. **Proportion of pupils with severe learning difficulties in primary and lower secondary education by location and by country**

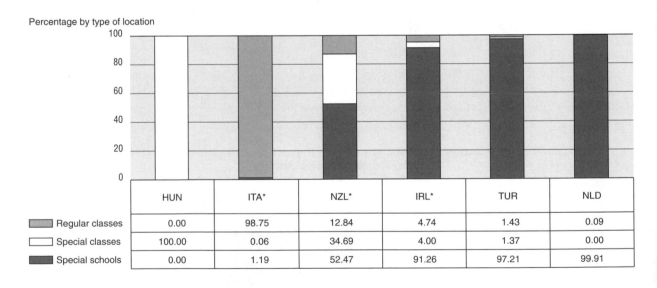

Percentage by type of location

	HUN	ITA*	NZL*	IRL*	TUR	NLD
Regular classes	0.00	98.75	12.84	4.74	1.43	0.09
Special classes	100.00	0.06	34.69	4.00	1.37	0.00
Special schools	0.00	1.19	52.47	91.26	97.21	99.91

* Public institutions only.
Italy: special schools are public and private.
Netherlands: figures in regular classes are estimates.
New Zealand: special schools are public and private.

Moderate learning difficulties

Of the countries supplying data, six maintain a category for students experiencing moderate learning difficulties and as can be seen from Chart 4.11 the proportions varies substantially from country to country. The lowest percentage being in New Zealand (0.03%) and the highest in Ireland (1.03%). This means that some coun-

OECD 2000

tries register 34.3 times as many as others. However, if the extremes are removed the variation between countries is substantially reduced with Italy (0.92%) registering only 3.4 times as many as Turkey (0.27%).

Chart 4.11 shows that three countries use regular classes, special classes and special schools for educating students in this category; Ireland (12.81%, 32.97%, 54.22%), Finland (1.21%, 30.61%, 68.18%), Turkey (49.86%, 48.19%, 1.95%). Italy uses regular classes (99.91%) and special schools (0.09%), in Hungary special classes (30.21%) and special schools (69.79%) are used whilst New Zealand places all of these students in special schools. In Switzerland the vast majority of those students are educated in special schools but missing data disallows the calculation of the proportions in each location.

At the extremes, the provision for these students varies then between their education being provided almost completely in regular schools to segregation in special schools.

Chart 4.11. **Proportion of pupils with moderate learning difficulties in primary and lower secondary education by location and by country**

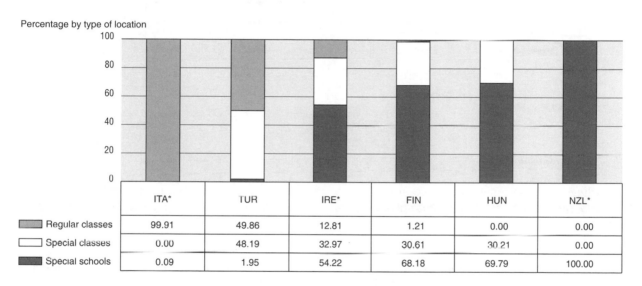

Percentage by type of location

	ITA*	TUR	IRE*	FIN	HUN	NZL*
Regular classes	99.91	49.86	12.81	1.21	0.00	0.00
Special classes	0.00	48.19	32.97	30.61	30.21	0.00
Special schools	0.09	1.95	54.22	68.18	69.79	100.00

* Public institutions only.
New Zealand: special schools are government-dependent private institutions.

Light learning difficulties

Chart 4.1K shows that three countries register students with light learning difficulties. Although no country actually uses this particular term, after having identified those in this report who are placed in the severe, moderate and learning disability categories there remained a fourth learning difficulty category which required a name in English. Light learning difficulty is used here to cover this group of students and it includes in Austria Category 1 learning disabilities, in Finland Category 1 mild mental impairment, and in the Netherlands Category 10 children with special needs/learning disabilities. National definitions allowing for a more formal comparison were not made available. There is less variation between countries for this category than for many of the others.

As Chart 4.12 shows, regular classes, special classes and special schools are used by Austria (32.07% estimated, 10.82%, 57.11%) and Finland (5.23%, 23.28%, 71.49%). In the Netherlands all of these students are in special schools.

Chart 4.12. **Proportion of pupils with light learning difficulties in primary and lower secondary education by location and by country**

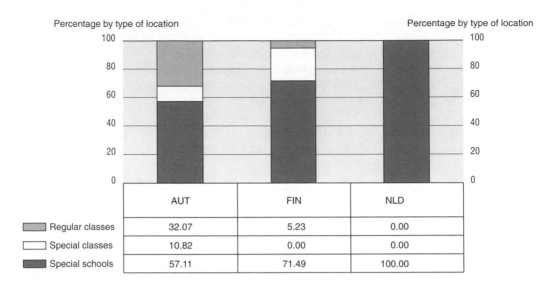

	AUT	FIN	NLD
Regular classes	32.07	5.23	0.00
Special classes	10.82	0.00	0.00
Special schools	57.11	71.49	100.00

Note: Only countries in which a clear LLD category exists.
Austria: data are estimated.

Learning disabilities

Chart 4.1L shows that only five countries have a category for students with learning disabilities and as for many of the other categories there is substantial variation among countries, the highest proportion being in Finland (11.17%) which registers 30.2 times as many as in Ireland (0.37%)

Chart 4.13. **Proportion of pupils with learning disabilities in primary and lower secondary education by location and by country**

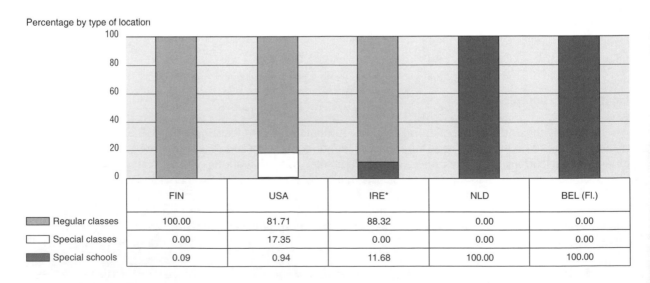

	FIN	USA	IRE*	NLD	BEL (Fl.)
Regular classes	100.00	81.71	88.32	0.00	0.00
Special classes	0.00	17.35	0.00	0.00	0.00
Special schools	0.09	0.94	11.68	100.00	100.00

* Public institutions only.
Note: Only countries in which a clear LD category exists.

OECD 2000

Chart 4.13 shows that regular classes, special classes and special schools are used in the United States (81.70%, 17.35%, 0.94%).

In Ireland they are shared between regular classes (88.32%) and special schools (11.68%). In Finland all of these students are in regular classes while in Belgium (Flemish Community) and in the Netherlands they are all in special schools.

Variation in provision among countries

The data presented thus far has analysed the location of education for each country by category. Another way of summarising this data is to bring the categories together and to look at them by country. Table 4.1 does just this, and shows the extent of the variety of provision used in different countries where unconfounded data based on clear categorical descriptions are available. For instance Belgium (Flemish Community) and Germany use mainly special school provision for these categories of disabilities while countries such as Greece and Switzerland use a mixture of special schools and special classes. Other countries use special schools, special classes and regular classes to varying extents. The table also summarises the extent to which these various forms of provision are utilised.

Thus the table summarises a complex picture across OECD countries as a whole with regard to the provision being made for a substantial proportion of the school age population with the most significant learning and socialising difficulties.

Table 4.1. **Variety of provisions used in different countries**

Categories	Austria	Belgium (Flemish Community)	Germany	Finland	France	Greece	Ireland	Italy	Netherlands	Portugal	Spain	CH Switzerland	Czech Republic	Hungary	Turkey	United States	New Zealand
Blind & visually impaired	S r	S r	S*	s R	S r	S c	s R	s R	S r	s R	s R	S*	S c r	S*	S r	s c R	s R
Deaf & hearing impaired	S r	S r	S*	S c r	S r	S c	s c R	s c R	S r	s c R	s R	S*	S c r	S*	S c r	s c R	s c R
Emotional & behavioural difficulties	S c r	S*	S*	s C r	S*	C*	s R		S r	R*	s R	s C	s c R			s c r	s c R
Severe learning difficulties					S*		S c	s c R	S			S*		C*	S c r	s c r	s c r
Moderate learning difficulties				S c r	S r		S c r	s R				S*			S c	s c r	S*
Light learning difficulties	S c r			S c r					S*								
Learning disabilities		S*		R*			s R		S*							s c R	
Physically handicapped	S c r	S r	S*	S c r	S r	S c	s c R	s R	S r		s R	S c	s c R	S c	s R	s c R	s C r
Multiple disabilities	S c r		S*		S*		S c r	S c	S r		S r	S*	S c r			s c r	
Speech & language disabilities	S r		S*		S*		c R		S r			S c	S c r		s c R	R*	C*
Hospital	S*	S*	S*						S r			S*	S*		S*		S*

s = special schools 10-50%
S = special schools 50-99%
S* = special schools 100%

c= special classes 10-50%
C = special classes 50-99%
C* = special classes 100%

r = regular classes 10-50%
R = regular classes 50-99%
R* = regular classes 100%

Further discussion of students experiencing difficulties in learning

The data reviewed thus far reveal two major patterns. First, categories for collecting statistical data vary considerably from country to country and second, it is clear that different definitions of the categories are in use. Furthermore, the data are often incomplete and taken together these factors comparisons between countries very difficult.

Table 4.2. **Classification of learning difficulties/disabilities including emotional and behavioral difficulties, and multiple disabilities**

	W-LD (up to IQ 50)	X-LD (up to IQ 70)	Y-LD (up to IQ 85)	Z-LD (more than IQ 85)	EBD	MD
Austria	Moderate or severe mental retardation		Learning disabilities		Emotional/behavioural problems	Children with multiple disabilities
Belgium (Flemish Community)	Type 2: Moderate or serious mental handicap		Type 1: Minor mental handicap	Type 8: Serious learning disabilities	Type 3: Serious emotional and/or behavioural problems	
Czech Republic	Mentally retarded				Developmental behaviour and learning problems	Multiple handicaps
Finland	N.B. Not in the educational system	Moderate mental impairment	Mild mental impairment	Specific learning disabilities. Support teaching (x)	Emotional and social impairment	
Germany	Mentally handicapped		Students with learning handicaps		Disturbed in behaviour, conduct	Multiple handicaps
Greece	Mentally retarded Autistics (x)		Learning difficulties			
Hungary	Trainable mental retardation	Educable mental retardation		Other disabilities		
Ireland	Severely and profoundly mentally handicapped. Moderate mental handicap.	Mild mental handicap		Specific learning disability. Pupils in need of remedial teaching (x)	Emotionally disturbed/behavioural disorders. Severely emotional/behavioural disorders	Multiply handicapped
Italy	Severe mental handicap	Moderate mental handicap				Multiple handicap
Netherlands	Profound mentally handicap or severe learning disabilities.		Children with SEN or learning disabilities	Learning disabilities	Deviant behaviour	Multiply handicapped
New Zealand	Intellectual disabilities-schools.	Intellectual disabilities-units and teachers	Learning difficulties Slow learners combined with emotional and behavioural difficulties		Emotional and/or behaviour difficulties/disorders. Students with severe social difficulties. Behaviour problems.	

Table 4.2. **Classification of learning difficulties/disabilities including emotional and behavioral difficulties, and multiple disabilities** (*cont.*)

	W-LD (up to IQ 50)	X-LD (up to IQ 70)	Y-LD (up to IQ 85)	Z-LD (more than IQ 85)	EBD	MD
Portugal	Mental disability		Specific learning difficulties		Emotional instability/disturbance	
Spain	Mental handicap				Emotional/behavioural problems	Multiple impairment
Switzerland	Trainable mental handicap	Educable mental handicap	Learning disabilities/introductory classes. Learning disabilities/special classes. Learning disabilities/vocationally oriented classes.		Behaviour disorders. Behavioural difficulties.	Multiply handicapped. Multiple disabilities.
Turkey	Trainable mentally handicapped	Educable mentally handicapped				
United States	Mental retardation. Multiple disabilities. Traumatic brain injury. Autism (x).	Mental retardation.		Specific learning difficulties	Emotional disturbance	Deaf/blindness. Multiple disabilities.

x = category included elsewhere.
EBD = emotional & behavioural difficulties
MD = multiple disabilities
W-LD = severe learning difficulties
X-LD = moderate learning difficulties
Y-LD = light learning difficulties
Z-LD = learning disabilities

Chart 4.14. **Cumulation of the number of students across certain disability categories expressed as a percentage of students in primary and lower secondary education**

EBD = emotional & behavioural difficulties; MD = multiple disabilities; W-LD = severe learning difficulties; X-LD = moderate learning difficulties; Y-LD = light learning difficulties; Z-LD = learning disabilities

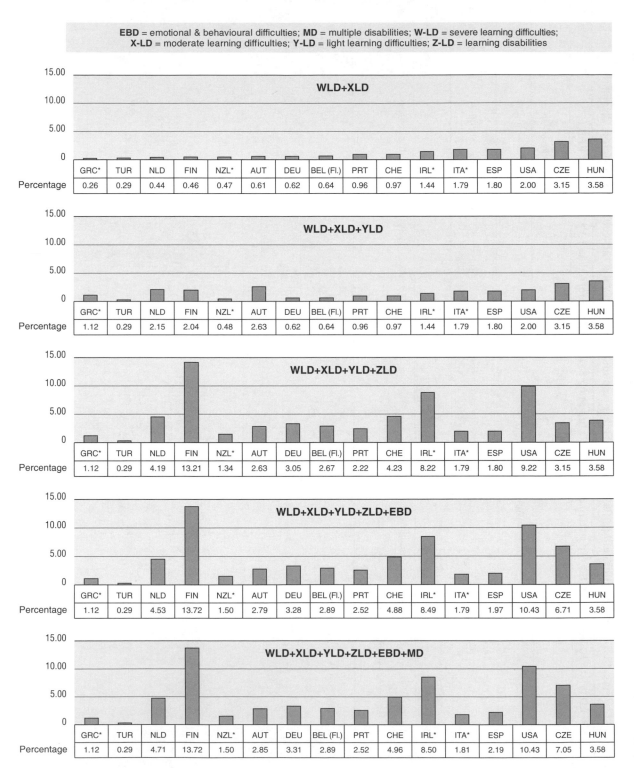

WLD+XLD

	GRC*	TUR	NLD	FIN	NZL*	AUT	DEU	BEL (Fl.)	PRT	CHE	IRL*	ITA*	ESP	USA	CZE	HUN
Percentage	0.26	0.29	0.44	0.46	0.47	0.61	0.62	0.64	0.96	0.97	1.44	1.79	1.80	2.00	3.15	3.58

WLD+XLD+YLD

	GRC*	TUR	NLD	FIN	NZL*	AUT	DEU	BEL (Fl.)	PRT	CHE	IRL*	ITA*	ESP	USA	CZE	HUN
Percentage	1.12	0.29	2.15	2.04	0.48	2.63	0.62	0.64	0.96	0.97	1.44	1.79	1.80	2.00	3.15	3.58

WLD+XLD+YLD+ZLD

	GRC*	TUR	NLD	FIN	NZL*	AUT	DEU	BEL (Fl.)	PRT	CHE	IRL*	ITA*	ESP	USA	CZE	HUN
Percentage	1.12	0.29	4.19	13.21	1.34	2.63	3.05	2.67	2.22	4.23	8.22	1.79	1.80	9.22	3.15	3.58

WLD+XLD+YLD+ZLD+EBD

	GRC*	TUR	NLD	FIN	NZL*	AUT	DEU	BEL (Fl.)	PRT	CHE	IRL*	ITA*	ESP	USA	CZE	HUN
Percentage	1.12	0.29	4.53	13.72	1.50	2.79	3.28	2.89	2.52	4.88	8.49	1.79	1.97	10.43	6.71	3.58

WLD+XLD+YLD+ZLD+EBD+MD

	GRC*	TUR	NLD	FIN	NZL*	AUT	DEU	BEL (Fl.)	PRT	CHE	IRL*	ITA*	ESP	USA	CZE	HUN
Percentage	1.12	0.29	4.71	13.72	1.50	2.85	3.31	2.89	2.52	4.96	8.50	1.81	2.19	10.43	7.05	3.58

* Public institutions only.
Austria and the Netherlands: data are estimated for children in regular classes.
See Table 4.2. for further explanation.

These points not withstanding, the data show large differences in apparent prevalences among countries, and it is not easy to understand why OECD countries with their inherent homogeneity should show such large discrepancies especially with regard to students who might be considered to be either casualties of pre-, peri-, or post-natal influences, or of random fluctuations of the normal distribution and other accidents of life. Bearing these points in mind, if these difficulties are "purely" biological in nature then roughly equivalent proportions of students identified might be expected among countries, and the differences observed here, it might be argued, are due to the differences in the definitions in use between countries.

One way of testing this hypothesis is to systematically cumulate the categories of students said to have various forms of learning difficulty where major differences due to definition are likely to be most evident. If the differences observed within the specific categories are due to definitional disparities then by accumulating the data across categories this effect should be lessened and the variation between countries commensurately reduced. Chart 4.14 shows what happens if this is carried out. The first chart shows the summation of the severe and moderate learning difficulty categories; the second adds on to these, those in the light learning difficulty category; the third adds those in the learning disabilities category and the fourth adds in those with emotional and behavioural problems, since for many countries this large category can become confounded with the problems of learning difficulty. The fifth rounds out the picture by including those with multiple disabilities. Table 4.2 provides the analysis through which national categories have been placed into six collective categories.

Inspection of Chart 4.14 suggests that there is little evening out of the variation between countries. This difference is maintained when the multiple disabilities category is added, as shown in the final chart. Thus this methodological process provides no convincing evidence that the differences observed in the single categories are due to definitional differences between countries. Furthermore, there is little support for the idea that there is a single aetiological basis to the learning difficulties identified.

Instead other factors must remain involved and as suggested in OECD (1995) these are likely to be at the level of policy and practices in education with regard to arrangements concerned with issues such as funding, placement, assessment, curriculum and pedagogy and training and the expectations this process produces in teachers. Differential rates of poverty will also be linked to variations in neo-natal and infantile morbidity, and this may be a further explanatory factor.

Conclusions

This chapter has considered the data based on the national categories of disability as supplied by participating countries. It has looked at the proportions registered in educational statistics by category and by location of education. The data show substantial variation in categories used by countries and in the country prevalence rates for the basic school years covering primary and lower secondary education. Furthermore, the location of education, regular schools, special classes, or special schools varies greatly from country to country. For almost all categories at the extremes the education experiences of similar students would be vastly different in different countries. For instance, in one they might be educated in regular classes while in another they may be fully segregated from mainstream education.

Substantial differences in definitions with regard to these categories also exist, and a procedure of adding together categories where different diagnoses might have been made as a result of the different definitions in use was developed in order to test whether the extent of the between country differences would be reduced. In the event no essential change could be observed and the interpretation remains that the origin of the differences is complex and multi-dimensional involving at least epidemiological, medical and educational policy and practice as well as socio-cultural mechanisms.

As far as international comparisons are concerned for educational policy-making, although they are not without relevance, these differences make interpretation very difficult and what is required is a simpler model which will provide more comparable data.

The additional problem of the concept of special educational needs which is being widely used internationally, further complicates the picture and has been discussed in Chapter 1. It, too, has no universal meaning and covers very different populations in different countries.

For these reasons the present study has adopted a simplified tri-partite cross-national categorisation, referred to as A, B and C within the context of a resources model which has been outlined in previous chapters. The following chapters use this framework to describe the remainder of the data gathered by the quantitative part of the instrument.

Chapter 5

ANALYSIS OF THE QUANTITATIVE DATA FOR CROSS-NATIONAL CATEGORIES A, B & C

Background

In addition to the data on categories of disability discussed in Chapter 4, information about the quantitative aspects of provision for students with special educational needs was obtained by further analysis of the data collection tables. The amount of information which countries were able to provide varied widely from country to country. There was an overall trend for the most detailed information to be available about provision in special schools, for substantially less information about special classes in regular or mainstream schools, and for there to be very patchy data on students fully integrated in regular classes in regular schools. Similarly there are more extensive and reliable data for students in cross-national Category A (relating broadly to what might be called organic defects relating to sensory, motor, or neurological systems) than for the other two cross-national categories.

While there is naturally most interest in analysing the information which is currently available, it is also of value to delineate those aspects where little or no data are at present collected at national level. This will help in focusing future data collection exercises on areas where it is reasonable to expect that good quality information will be available. It will also highlight features seen to be central to obtaining indicators of the functioning of national systems in respect of students with special educational needs, but where data are not currently generally available. Study of those few countries which do manage to collect relevant information may provide pointers to ways in which other countries might modify or extend their own data collection exercises to generate similar information.

Hence the following sections are structured to provide an analysis of current data, concentrating on areas where its quantity and quality appear acceptable. However, attention is also given to areas where data are much more patchy, or even practically non-existent.

Numbers of students with special educational needs

Countries were asked to provide data in terms of the resources definition of special educational needs (see in Chapter 1, "Operational definitions of cross-national categories"). The numbers of students they reported as falling within this definition expressed as a percentage of the overall school population in each country are presented in the data bars of Chart 5.1 broken down into cross-national categories A, B and C.

As may be seen from Chart 5.1, the proportions of students receiving additional resources are reported to be very different. 33.53% are additionally supported in the Netherlands in contrast to 0.41% in Turkey *i.e.* 81.78 times as many.

These figures differ in some cases from the percentages which would have been obtained if national definitions of special educational needs had been employed rather than the resources definition (see Chart 5.2). In Hungary, for example, 5.1% of students fall within the national categories definition, but a further 11.1% receive additional resources making 16.2% overall. However it should be stressed that in nearly half of the countries where the data permit the comparison, the resources and national definitions provide identical statistics.

Chart 5.1. **Students receiving additional resources to access the curriculum as a percentage of all students in primary and lower secondary education, by cross-national categories (based on head counts), 1996**

N.B. The chart includes countries where resources definition and national categories definition are equivalent.
The chart includes countries where resources definition and national categories definition are equivalent.

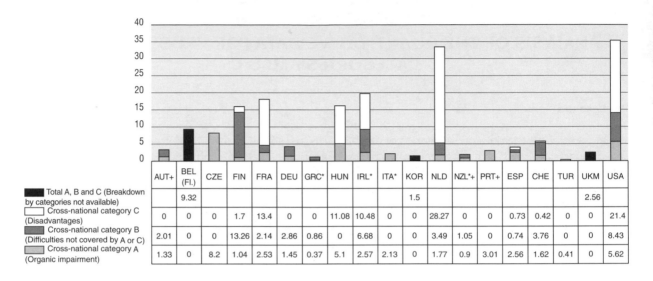

	AUT+	BEL (Fl.)	CZE	FIN	FRA	DEU	GRC*	HUN	IRL*	ITA*	KOR	NLD	NZL*+	PRT+	ESP	CHE	TUR	UKM	USA
■ Total A, B and C (Breakdown by categories not available)		9.32									1.5							2.56	
□ Cross-national category C (Disadvantages)	0	0	0	1.7	13.4	0	0	11.08	10.48	0	0	28.27	0	0	0.73	0.42	0	0	21.4
▓ Cross-national category B (Difficulties not covered by A or C)	2.01	0	0	13.26	2.14	2.86	0.86	0	6.68	0	0	3.49	1.05	0	0.74	3.76	0	0	8.43
▒ Cross-national category A (Organic impairment)	1.33	0	8.2	1.04	2.53	1.45	0.37	5.1	2.57	2.13	0	1.77	0.9	3.01	2.56	1.62	0.41	0	5.62

* Greece, Ireland, Italy and New Zealand: public institutions only.
+ Cross national category C not available. Cross national category B not available for Portugal.

Austria, New Zealand, Portugal: national categories data reported, additional resources are provided for other categories but data are missing. The data in regular classes are estimates.
Belgium (Flemish Community): includes upper secondary students (ISCED 3).
France: estimated figures (primary education only for the national categories in special classes in regular schools and regular classes in regular schools).
Hungary: some students in upper secondary education are also included.
Ireland: estimated figures.
Netherlands: note that the percentage of students in cross-national category C is much lower in lower secondary education than in primary education.
Turkey: Turkish data refer only to compulsory school period (ISCED 1).

As noted, in many other countries the resources definition figure substantially exceeds that which the national definition would have provided. The differences are most marked in data relating to regular class settings where for example Hungary gave a total of 132 145 students within the resources definition in regular classes against 13 476 within the national definition. Similarly, Spain gives figures of 136 437 and 80 041 respectively. Such differences reflect a situation where certain categories of students are regarded as falling outside the national definition but within the resources definition. Chart 5.2 contrasts the resources definition (dark bars) with the national categories (light bars) where data is available.

It appears likely that using the resources definition is going some way to achieving its objective of increasing the comparability of national statistics. Countries with relatively narrow national definitions of special educational needs, when using the resources definition, are including categories of students that are included by those countries using wider national definitions of special educational needs.

There is, of course, no guarantee that different countries are using the resources definition in exactly the same way, although every effort was made in rubrics accompanying the data collection instrument to give a detailed explication of the meaning of resources to be used. It will be a task for subsequent uses of the instrument to identify any likely anomalies and to seek ways of getting rid of them in order to improve data quality.

Chart 5.2. **Number of students with special educational needs as a percentage of all primary and lower secondary school age children by national categories and resources models**

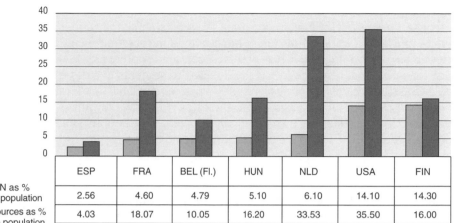

	ESP	FRA	BEL (Fl.)	HUN	NLD	USA	FIN
A1. National categories of SEN as % of compulsory school age population	2.56	4.60	4.79	5.10	6.10	14.10	14.30
A2. SEN according to the resources as % of compulsory school age population	4.03	18.07	10.05	16.20	33.53	35.50	16.00

Belgium (Flemish Community): includes upper secondary students (ISCED 3).
France: estimated figures.
United States: number in resource model is estimated.

Chart 5.3 shows how the total number of students shown in Chart 5.1 are split between the three settings of special schools, special classes in regular mainstream schools, and regular classes in mainstream schools. In 11 of the 16 countries for which comparative data are available, the largest proportions of students are educated in the integrated setting of regular classes, although both the relative and absolute numbers of students in the settings vary considerably.

Chart 5.3. **Number of students with special educational needs within resources definition as a percentage of all students in primary and lower secondary education by location and by country**

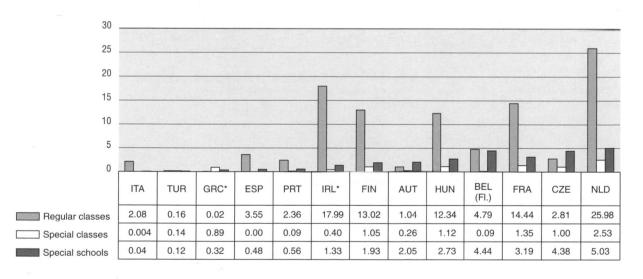

	ITA	TUR	GRC*	ESP	PRT	IRL*	FIN	AUT	HUN	BEL (Fl.)	FRA	CZE	NLD
Regular classes	2.08	0.16	0.02	3.55	2.36	17.99	13.02	1.04	12.34	4.79	14.44	2.81	25.98
Special classes	0.004	0.14	0.89	0.00	0.09	0.40	1.05	0.26	1.12	0.09	1.35	1.00	2.53
Special schools	0.04	0.12	0.32	0.48	0.56	1.33	1.93	2.05	2.73	4.44	3.19	4.38	5.03

*Public institutions only.
Austria: the data in regular classes are estimates.
Belgium (Flemish Community): includes upper secondary students (ISCED 3).
France: estimated figures.
Italy: special classes and regular classes are public institutions only.
Turkey: data refer only to compulsory school period (ISCED 1).

Cross-national categories A, B & C

Discussion of the quantitative data produced by this data collection exercise is initially structured in terms of the three cross-national categories. Chart 5.4 shows that there is wide variation in the relative use of these categories by different countries. At one extreme, the Netherlands have over three-quarters of students to whom additional resources are provided in cross-national Category C (broadly speaking students viewed as disadvantaged because of socio-economic or other factors). At the other extreme, Turkey and Italy provide additional resources almost exclusively to students in cross-national Category A. It appears reasonable to assume that all countries have within their educational system students who are disadvantaged by one or more aspects of their background to the extent to which they find difficulties in accessing the regular curriculum. This suggests that Turkey and Italy apparently are not providing additional resources to students who in other countries (such as the Netherlands) would receive them.

Chart 5.4. **Number of students with special educational needs within resources definition in cross-national categories A, B and C as a percentage of the total numbers in A, B and C by countries**

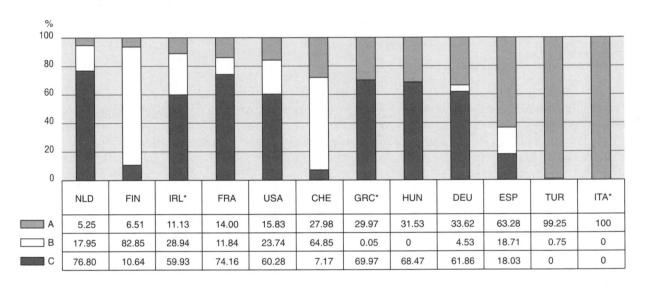

	NLD	FIN	IRL*	FRA	USA	CHE	GRC*	HUN	DEU	ESP	TUR	ITA*
A	5.25	6.51	11.13	14.00	15.83	27.98	29.97	31.53	33.62	63.28	99.25	100
B	17.95	82.85	28.94	11.84	23.74	64.85	0.05	0	4.53	18.71	0.75	0
C	76.80	10.64	59.93	74.16	60.28	7.17	69.97	68.47	61.86	18.03	0	0

* Public institutions only.
France and the United States: estimated figures.
Switzerland: this maybe underestimated, for example in the Canton of Zurich 12% of all school children receive support because of their low performance in German or Math. These figures are not reflected in the Federal statistics.
Turkey: data refer only to compulsory school period (ISCED 1).

Alternative explanations are, of course, possible. It may be that additional resources are being made available to such students but that, perhaps because of difficulties in assessing or conceptualising these resources, they have not been included in the data tables.

There are also large differences from country to country in the relative proportions of students considered to fall within cross-national Category B. Two countries, Hungary and Italy, have no students in this category and Turkey less than 1%. In Finland they account for over 80% of students falling within the resources definition and in Switzerland they are almost two-thirds of these students. Cross-national Category B refers to students who receive additional resources because of difficulties in accessing the regular curriculum for reasons not obviously ascribable to either organic defects or to disadvantages accruing from their background; including for example students with behavioural or emotional difficulties and in a few countries students who are exceptionally gifted or talented.

Similar arguments to those presented in relation to the relative lack of students in cross-national Category C in some countries might also be put forward for these students. However, while it would be anticipated that all educational systems would have students with, for instance, emotional and behavioural difficulties, providing additional resources for their education is perhaps only one of a number of possible strategies to help them. It might be argued that certain forms of educational provision or approaches to curriculum would be less likely to promote emotional or behavioural difficulties in students, or to assist students with such difficulties in accessing the regular curriculum. Hence the lack of students in cross-national Category B, while it might indicate that there are students with difficulties not receiving additional resources, could possibly suggest that such difficulties are being met in other ways.

Again, the possibility exists that this is a statistical artefact arising from an inability or unwillingness to include data relating to cross-national Category B because of difficulties in its collection, always bearing in mind that many students who might be viewed as falling within this category are likely to be educated in mainstream schools where there is a general finding that national data relevant to special educational needs are more difficult to collect than in special schools.

Quantitative data on cross-national Category A

Cross-national Category A, as discussed and defined in Chapter 1 (see "Operational definitions of cross-national categories"), roughly corresponds to needs arising from impairing conditions. All countries using categorical systems for special educational needs have national categories which they consider to fall within cross-national Category A, although the number of such categories varies widely from country to country (see Table 3.2). Chart 5.5 shows the percentage of students within primary and lower secondary education considered to fall within this category for different countries. Chart 5.6 shows, where data is available, the proportions of students with special educational needs as described through national categories (grey bars), the resources model (black bars) and cross-national Category A (white bars).

Chart 5.5. **Number of students in cross-national Category A as a percentage of all students in primary and lower secondary education**

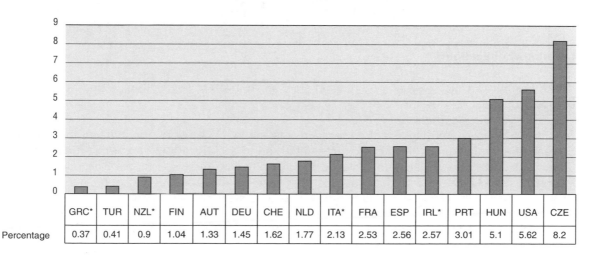

	GRC*	TUR	NZL*	FIN	AUT	DEU	CHE	NLD	ITA*	FRA	ESP	IRL*	PRT	HUN	USA	CZE
Percentage	0.37	0.41	0.9	1.04	1.33	1.45	1.62	1.77	2.13	2.53	2.56	2.57	3.01	5.1	5.62	8.2

* Public institutions only.
France and the United States: estimated figures
Turkey: data refer only to compulsory school period (ISCED 1).

OECD 2000

Chart 5.6. **Number of students with special educational needs as a percentage of all students in primary and lower secondary education, by national categories, resources models and in cross-national Category A**

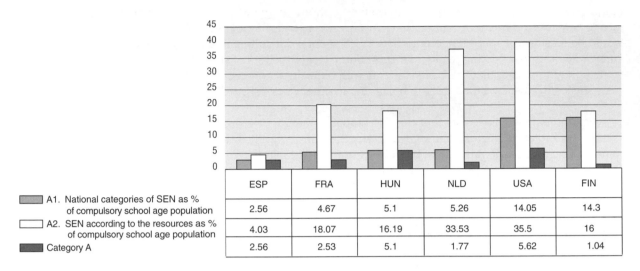

	ESP	FRA	HUN	NLD	USA	FIN
A1. National categories of SEN as % of compulsory school age population	2.56	4.67	5.1	5.26	14.05	14.3
A2. SEN according to the resources as % of compulsory school age population	4.03	18.07	16.19	33.53	35.5	16
Category A	2.56	2.53	5.1	1.77	5.62	1.04

France, Spain and the United States (A2): estimated figures.

It reveals that although wide variation continues to exist between countries in terms of Category A students, the differences are substantially less than that revealed by the gross figures estimated via either national categories or the resources model and very substantially less than the differences between countries for some individual categories discussed in the previous chapter. This confirms the use of the A category as part of the tri-partite approach and increases confidence that like is being compared with like. However, large differences still remain that require explanation. For example there are 5.4 times as many students in Category "A" in the United States (5.62%) in contrast to Finland (1.04%).

Location of education

The extent to which Category A students are educated within segregated settings also varies widely between countries as shown in Chart 5.7.

Chart 5.8 shows the numbers of students in cross-national Category A in different locations as a percentage of all students within the resources definition in each location. Thus while it can be seen from Chart 5.6 that in the Netherlands, for instance, 87.41% of students in cross-national Category "A" are educated in special schools, "A" students only account for 30.59% of the students in those schools as revealed in Chart 5.8. In contrast, while Italy has almost 98% of its students in cross-national Category A in regular classes in regular schools and fewer than 2% in special schools, all of the students in special schools are in this cross-national category (not in itself surprising, as all Italian students within the resources definition are considered to be in cross-national Category A).

It is clear from the analyses that students who are thought to have learning difficulties because of impairments receive very different treatments in different countries; a finding essentially independent of the proportions placed in Category A.

Chart 5.7. **Proportion of students in cross-national Category A by location**

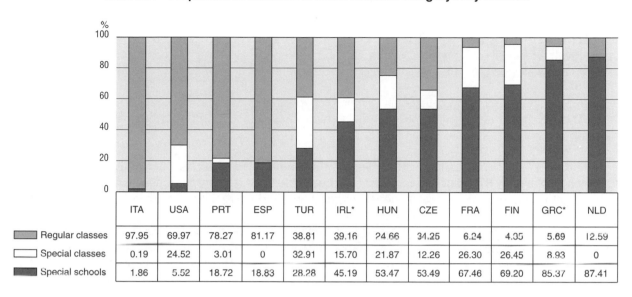

	ITA	USA	PRT	ESP	TUR	IRL*	HUN	CZE	FRA	FIN	GRC*	NLD
Regular classes	97.95	69.97	78.27	81.17	38.81	39.16	24.66	34.25	6.24	4.35	5.69	12.59
Special classes	0.19	24.52	3.01	0	32.91	15.70	21.87	12.26	26.30	26.45	8.93	0
Special schools	1.86	5.52	18.72	18.83	28.28	45.19	53.47	53.49	67.46	69.20	85.37	87.41

* Public institutions only.
France and the United States: estimated figures.
Italy: special classes and regular classes are public institutions only.
Netherlands: the data for regular classes are estimated.
Turkey: data refer only to compulsory school period (ISCED 1).

Chart 5.8. **Number of students in cross-national Category A in different locations as a percentage of all students within the resources definition in that location**

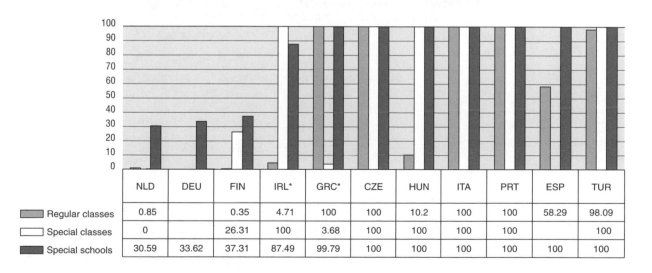

	NLD	DEU	FIN	IRL*	GRC*	CZE	HUN	ITA	PRT	ESP	TUR
Regular classes	0.85		0.35	4.71	100	100	10.2	100	100	58.29	98.09
Special classes	0		26.31	100	3.68	100	100	100	100		100
Special schools	30.59	33.62	37.31	87.49	99.79	100	100	100	100	100	100

*Public institutions only.
France: estimated figures.
Italy: special classes and regular classes are public institutions only.
Turkey: data refer only to compulsory school period (ISCED 1).

Quantitative data on cross-national Category B

As previously discussed the quantity and quality of data relating to cross-national categories B and C are inferior to that for cross-national Category A. Cross-national Category B, as discussed and defined in Chapter 1, is effectively a residual category covering those national categories referring to students whose special needs are not clearly ascribed to either organic defects or disadvantages in their socio-economic background.

While all countries using categorical systems for special educational needs have national categories which they consider to fall within cross-national Category A, several countries placed no categories in cross-national Category B (see Table 3.2 in Chapter 3 for details).

Chart 5.9 shows the percentages of students within primary and lower secondary education considered to fall within Category B for different countries, and Chart 5.10 shows the proportions of B (white bars) in comparison to those in the national categories (light grey bars), and the resources model (dark grey bars).

Chart 5.4 presented data on the percentage of students falling within cross-national Category B relative to those in the other two cross-national categories. The wide variation across countries for all of these measures is again noteworthy. As may be expected in a residual category, those in cross-national Category B represent a wide range of students, varying from those with emotional and behavioural disorders to the gifted and talented and this may reflect countries varying understanding of the concept of special education. At the least, cross-national Category B is useful as a means of reducing variance and increasing comparability between countries' databases and between their different classification schemes.

Location of education

The extent to which these students are educated within segregated settings also varies widely between countries as shown in Chart 5.11. Missing data for many of the national categories within cross-national Category B mean that it is only possible to provide comparative data for the three locations for the five coun-

Chart 5.9. **Number of students in cross-national Category B as a percentage of all students in primary and lower secondary education**

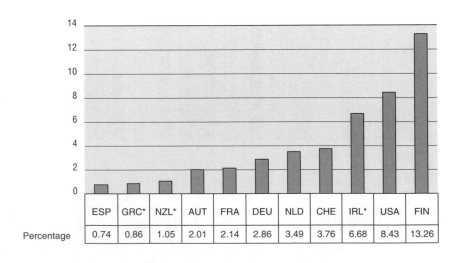

	ESP	GRC*	NZL*	AUT	FRA	DEU	NLD	CHE	IRL*	USA	FIN
Percentage	0.74	0.86	1.05	2.01	2.14	2.86	3.49	3.76	6.68	8.43	13.26

* Public institutions only.
France and the United States: estimated figures.

Chart 5.10.   **Number of students with special educational needs as a percentage of all students in primary and lower secondary education, by national categories, resources models and in cross-national Category B**

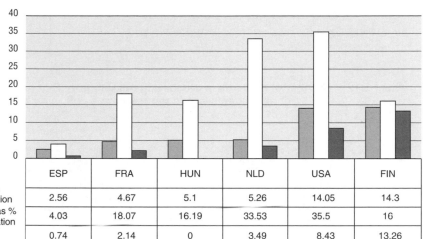

	ESP	FRA	HUN	NLD	USA	FIN
A1. National categories of SEN as % of compulsory school age population	2.56	4.67	5.1	5.26	14.05	14.3
A2. SEN according to the resources as % of compulsory school age population	4.03	18.07	16.19	33.53	35.5	16
Category B	0.74	2.14	0	3.49	8.43	13.26

France: estimated figures.
United States (A2): number in resource model is estimated.

Chart 5.11.   **Proportion of students in cross-national Category B by location**

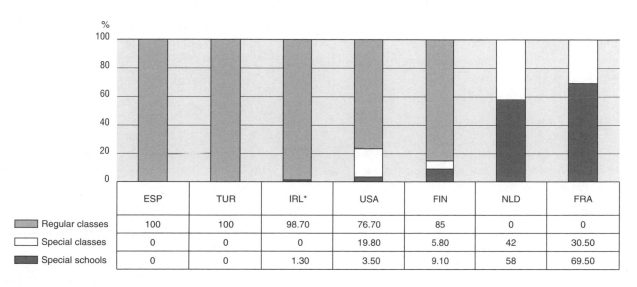

	ESP	TUR	IRL*	USA	FIN	NLD	FRA
Regular classes	100	100	98.70	76.70	85	0	0
Special classes	0	0	0	19.80	5.80	42	30.50
Special schools	0	0	1.30	3.50	9.10	58	69.50

* Public institutions only.
France and the United States: estimated figures.

OECD 2000

tries shown in the chart. It reveals great variation of education for these students. In France and the Netherlands all cross-national Category B's are in special schools or classes but in Finland, Ireland, Spain, Turkey, and the United States the vast majority are in regular classes.

Chart 5.12 shows the numbers of students in cross-national Category B in different locations as a percentage of all students within the resources definition in each location. However the data is too incomplete to allow for a clear interpretation.

Chart 5.12.   **Number of students in cross-national Category B in different locations as a percentage of all students within the resources definition in that location**

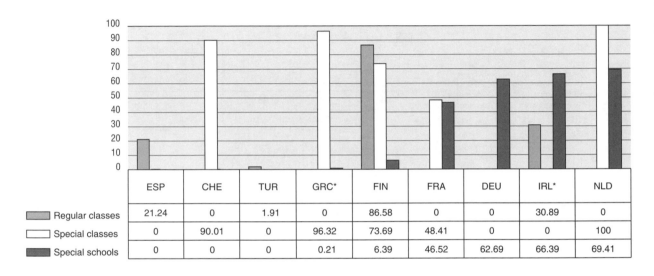

	ESP	CHE	TUR	GRC*	FIN	FRA	DEU	IRL*	NLD
Regular classes	21.24	0	1.91	0	86.58	0	0	30.89	0
Special classes	0	90.01	0	96.32	73.69	48.41	0	0	100
Special schools	0	0	0	0.21	6.39	46.52	62.69	66.39	69.41

*Public institutions only.
France: estimated figures.
Turkey: data refer only to compulsory school period (ISCED 1).

Quantitative data on cross-national Category C

Cross-national Category C, as discussed and defined in Chapter 1, covers those national categories referring to students considered to have special needs arising from disadvantages in their socio-economic background. Several countries had no categories which they placed in cross-national Category C (see Table 3.2 for details).

Overall numbers and percentages

Chart 5.13 shows the percentage of students within primary and lower secondary education considered to fall within this category for different countries. Chart 5.14 shows the proportions in C (white bars) in contrast to national categories definition of special educational needs (light grey bars) and the resources description (dark grey bars).

Chart 5.4 presented data on the percentage of students falling within cross-national Category C relative to those in the other two cross-national categories. The wide variation across countries for each of these measures is once again noteworthy and provides some indication of the difference in the extent to which countries provide extra resources for those students from disadvantaged backgrounds. A fuller understanding of this conclusion, however, demands a more detailed analysis of other factors *e.g.* the level of national funding for education, estimated extent of disadvantage in countries *e.g.* differences in immigration levels.

Chart 5.13. **Number of students in cross-national Category C as a percentage of all students in primary and lower secondary education**

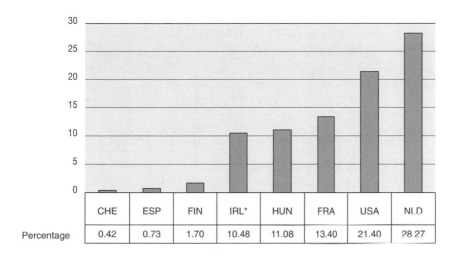

	CHE	ESP	FIN	IRL*	HUN	FRA	USA	NLD
Percentage	0.42	0.73	1.70	10.48	11.08	13.40	21.40	28.27

* Public institutions only.
France: estimated figures.
Switzerland: this figure is considerably underestimated.

Chart 5.14. **Number of students with special educational needs as a percentage of all students in primary and lower secondary education, by national categories, resources models and in cross-national Category C**

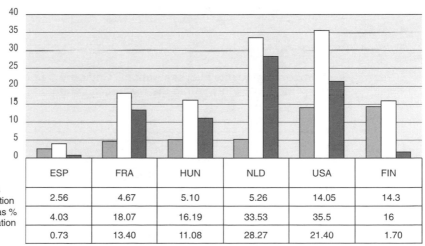

	ESP	FRA	HUN	NLD	USA	FIN
A1. National categories of SEN as % of compulsory school age population	2.56	4.67	5.10	5.26	14.05	14.3
A2. SEN according to the resources as % of compulsory school age population	4.03	18.07	16.19	33.53	35.5	16
Category C	0.73	13.40	11.08	28.27	21.40	1.70

France: estimated figures.
United States: cross-national categories C and A2 are estimated.

Location of education

On the basis of estimated data available, few students in cross-national Category C are educated in segregated settings. Chart 5.15 reveals that in those countries offering a comparison virtually all of these students are educated in regular classes.

Chart 5.15.   **Proportion of students in cross-national Category C by location**

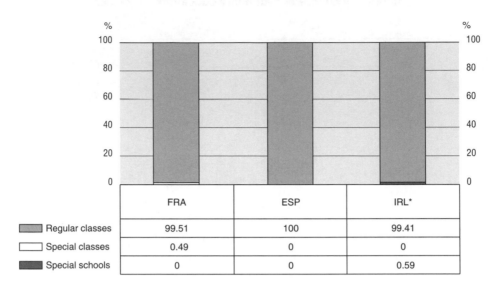

	FRA	ESP	IRL*
Regular classes	99.51	100	99.41
Special classes	0.49	0	0
Special schools	0	0	0.59

France, Ireland and Spain: estimated figures.
Ireland: public institutions only and data on children of refugees in regular classes are missing.

Chart 5.16 shows the numbers of students in cross-national Category C in different locations as percentages of all students within the resources definition in each location. As for cross-national Category B the data are too incomplete to draw any conclusions.

Chart 5.16.   **Number of students in cross-national Category C in different location as a percentage of all students within the resources definition in that location**

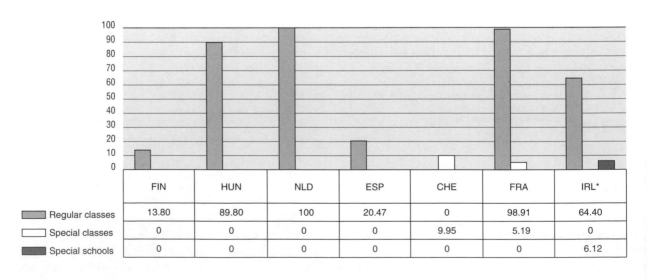

	FIN	HUN	NLD	ESP	CHE	FRA	IRL*
Regular classes	13.80	89.80	100	20.47	0	98.91	64.40
Special classes	0	0	0	0	9.95	5.19	0
Special schools	0	0	0	0	0	0	6.12

*Public institutions only.
France: estimated figures.

OECD 2000

Discussion and summary

This chapter has summarised the data obtained following the definition of special educational needs based on resources provided and the re-classification of the students identified into the tri-partite cross-national classification A, B and C.

Because of the variation in the use of the term special educational needs, the resources model has been developed to identify the fullest number of students receiving additional support with the aim of making more accurate comparisons between countries. The approach shows that the use of the resources model, for some countries in contrast to the use of national categories only, incorporates many more students. Countries seem to vary substantially in the extent to which extra resources are provided and the variation requires further exploration and explanation.

The "ABC" model provides a simpler approach to comparing students with special educational needs which avoids the medical categorical model described in Chapter 4. It is clear that A reduces the variance in the data in comparison to either the national categories or resources model thus giving greater confidence that like is being compared with like. Students falling into this group receive very different experiences in different countries, almost certainly because of different educational policies and practices in place. This conclusion supports that drawn in Chapter 4.

Data on Categories B and C are weak and reveal greater variability than for A. It would be unsafe to draw further conclusions until the data quality is improved.

OECD 2000

Chapter 6

ADDITIONAL ANALYSES OF THE QUANTITATIVE DATA

Introduction

This chapter focuses on what the data tables show about the different physical locations in which students with special educational needs are educated, following the simple categorisation of special schools, special classes in mainstream schools, and regular classes in regular schools employed in the previous chapter.

Several other aspects are also analysed including the gender ratios for students with special needs found in different settings and categorisations, student-staff ratios and the age distributions of these students in a number of national systems.

Special schools

The amount of segregated provision in the form of special schools differs widely from country to country. As Table 6.1 shows the number of such institutions expressed as a proportion of the total school population varies from 1.6 to 72.4 per 100 000 students. The table also shows that the average size of such schools varies substantially from 21.9 to 124.9. There appears to be little difference in average size of special schools at primary and lower secondary levels. In many countries the overwhelming proportion of special schools are publicly provided, but for four countries (Flemish Community of Belgium), Italy, Spain, and Switzerland) over half of the special schools are subsidised private.

Table 6.1. **Number and size of special schools**

	Number of special schools	Number relative to total school population**	Average size of special school	Percentage of private special schools
Austria	317	41.4	49.4	3.80
Belgium (Fl.)	313	31.4	124.9	65.81
Czech Republic	785	72.4	60.6	6.5
Finland	285	48.4	39.6	1.40
Germany	3397	37.4	115.1	15.70
Greece*	147	14.1	21.9	m
Hungary	271	25.3	107.8	1.10
Ireland*	119	21.0	63.3	0.00
Italy	71	1.6	24.5	0.30
Netherlands	946	48.0	m	m
Portugal	85	6.3	88.8	m
Spain	491	12.8	37.6	59.10
Switzerland	350	45.2	35.9	54.60
Turkey	128	2.0	58.6	4.70
United Kingdom	1565	21.1	73.1	7.00

* Public institutions only.
** Number of special schools per 100 000 of total primary and lower secondary school population.
Belgium (Flemish Community): includes upper secondary students (ISCED 3).
Finland: school year 1996.
Greek and Portuguese data refer to all national categories within national (not resources) definition.
Portuguese data refer only to schools coming under Ministry of Education (there are schools coming under Ministry of Solidarity and Social Assistance).
Turkey: Turkish data refer only to compulsory school period (ISCED 1).

OECD 2000

The relative proportions of male and female students in special schools are discussed in a separate section below.

Special classes

Data on special classes are sparse compared with that available on special schools. Eight countries provide information on the number of special classes for students with special educational needs. As shown in Table 6.2 class sizes are typically low, ranging from under 3 to nearly 14. For five countries information has been provided permitting the calculation of the average number of special classes per school showing a range from 1.36 to 3.53.

Gender ratios in special classes are also discussed separately below.

Table 6.2. **Special classes – Number per school and average size**

	Average number of special classes per school	Average size of special classes
Austria	1.64	6.93
Czech Republic	3.53	10.15
Finland	m	7.39
Greece	m	13.61
Ireland*	1.29	9.78
Italy*	2.48	3.46
Portugal	m	2.63
Turkey	1.36	11.01

*Public institutions only.
Portuguese data refer to all national categories within national (not resources) definition.

Regular classes

Information about the integrated provision made when students with special educational needs are educated in the same classes as other students is crucial in any assessment of this type of provision. Unfortunately, it appears that this kind of information is rarely available at national level when statistics are collected. In the current exercise only two countries, Italy and Turkey were able to provide relevant data as given in Table 6.3.

Table 6.3. **Number and percentage of regular classes with special needs students**

	Number of classes		Percentage of classes	
	Primary	Lower secondary	Primary	Lower secondary
Italy*	43 107	34 015	28.7	37.7
Turkey	5 251	303	1.98	0.56

* Public institutions only.
Turkish data refer only to compulsory school period (ISCED 1).

The data from Italy are interesting because of the policy of full inclusion. It shows that 28.7% of primary level classes, and 37.7% of lower secondary level classes have students with disabilities included in them. This figure is especially significant, since in Italy, all students identified are in cross-national Category A and will therefore be students with the most extensive needs.

Gender ratios for students with special educational needs in regular classes are discussed below.

Relative numbers of male and female students with special educational needs

While most countries do not have available information at national level about the gender of students with special educational needs within their system, sufficient countries do this for interesting comparisons to be made. Charts 6.1, 6.2 and 6.3 provide this information for special schools, special classes, and regular classes respectively.

Chart 6.1. **Gender ratios in special school**

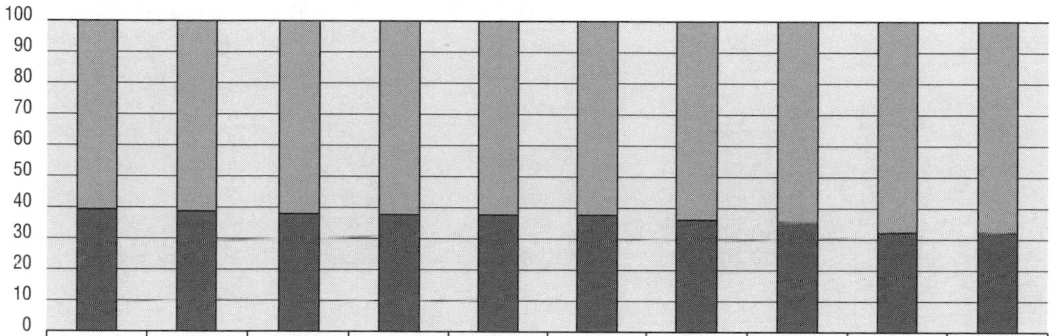

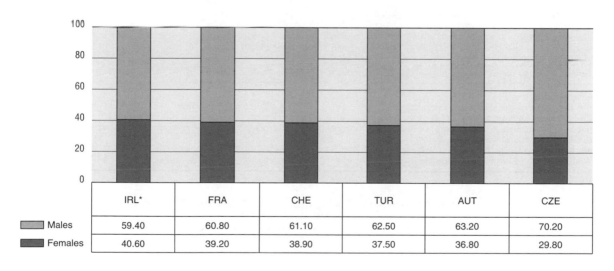

	ESP	FRA	BEL (Fl.)	AUT	IRL*	TUR	DEU	CHE	UKM	NLD
Males	60.60	61.30	62	62.10	62.10	62.10	63.60	64.20	67.80	67.70
Females	39.40	38.70	38	37.90	37.90	37.90	36.40	35.80	32.20	32.30

* Public institutions only.
France: estimated figures.
Turkey: data refer only to compulsory school period (ISCED 1).

Chart 6.2. **Gender ratios in special classes**

	IRL*	FRA	CHE	TUR	AUT	CZE
Males	59.40	60.80	61.10	62.50	63.20	70.20
Females	40.60	39.20	38.90	37.50	36.80	29.80

* Public institutions only.

A noteworthy feature of the data is the lack of variability across both countries and settings. Generally about 60% of special needs students are male, with a range from 60.6 to 67.7 in special schools; 59.4 to 70.2 in special classes; and 51.6 to 73.9 for students with special educational needs in regular schools. This remarkable degree of consistency in a data set, which in other respects shows very substantial variability between countries in almost all other measures, is largely maintained when other breakdowns of the data are calculated. Tables 6.4, 6.5 and 6.6 show corresponding data for the different locations separated out into the three cross-national categories. Tables 6.7, 6.8 and 6.9 provide gender ratios for students with visual, auditory and mental disabilities.

Chart 6.3. **Gender ratios of students with special educational needs in regular classes**

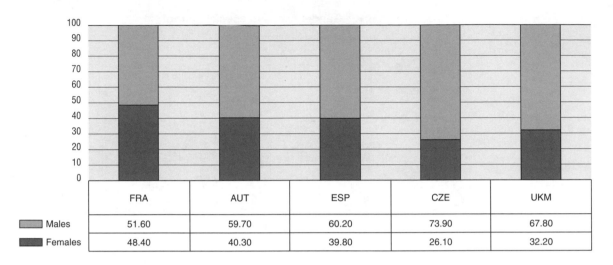

	FRA	AUT	ESP	CZE	UKM
Males	51.60	59.70	60.20	73.90	67.80
Females	48.40	40.30	39.80	26.10	32.20

France: estimated figures.

Table 6.4. **Gender ratios in cross-national Category A by location**
Percentage of males

	Special schools	Special classes	Regular classes
Austria	60.1	58.3	57.75
Czech Republic	m	70.2	73.2
Germany	62.3	m	m
Ireland*	60.7	62.7	m
Netherlands	67.63	m	m
Spain	60.6	m	60.6
Switzerland	64.3	m	m
Turkey	62.1	62.5	m

* Public institutions only.
Austria: regular classes figures are estimated.
Czech Republic: data are missing for Category 1 (mentally retarded) in regular classes.
Ireland: data are missing for Category 11 (severely & profoundly mentally handicapped) in special schools; data are missing for Category 7 (auditory handicap) in special classes.
Switzerland: data for special classes are included in those given for special schools.
Turkey: data are missing for Category 8 (chronically ill) in special schools; data refer only to compulsory school period (ISCED 1).

Table 6.5. **Gender ratios in cross-national Category B by location**
Percentage of males

	Special schools	Special classes	Regular classes
Austria	63.6	64.2	60.92
France	60.9	58.2	m
Germany	65.4	m	m
Ireland*	78.4	m	m
Netherlands	67.9	m	m
Spain	m	m	60.4
Switzerland	m	62	m

* Public institutions only.
Austria and Spain: regular classes figures are estimated.

Table 6.6. **Gender ratios in cross-national Category C by location**
Percentage of males

	Special schools	Special classes	Regular classes
France	m	54.4	51.3
Germany	64.2	m	m
Ireland*	66.8	m	49
Spain	m	m	59
Switzerland	m	53	m

* Public institutions only.
Ireland: regular classes figures are estimated.

Table 6.7. **Gender ratios for students with visual disabilities by location**
Percentage of males

	Special schools	Special classes	Regular classes
Austria	50.8	m	m
Czech Republic	m	47.6	55.7
Germany	57.7	m	m
Netherlands	58.9	m	m
Spain	58.9	m	58.9
Switzerland	63.8	m	m
Turkey	63.6	63.3	m

Switzerland: data for special classes are included in those given for special schools.
Turkey: data refer only to compulsory school period (ISCED 1).

Table 6.8. **Gender ratios for students with auditory disabilities by location**
Percentage of males

	Special schools	Special classes	Regular classes
Austria	58.6	m	m
Czech Republic	m	m	53.7
Germany	57.7	m	m
Ireland*	50.3	63	m
Netherlands	60.8	m	m
Spain	57.9	m	57.2
Switzerland	66.5	m	m
Turkey	59.4	61.9	m

*Public institutions only.
Germany and Switzerland: data for special classes are included in those given for special schools.
Turkey: data refer only to compulsory school period (ISCED 1).

Table 6.9. **Gender ratios for students with mental impairments/handicaps by location**
Percentage of males

	Special schools	Special classes	Regular classes
Austria	59.6	58.8	m
Czech Republic	m	58	70.3
Germany	61.7	m	m
Ireland*	61.5	61.6	m
Netherlands	66.5	m	m
Spain	59.6	m	60.7
Switzerland	61.5	61.1	m
Turkey	67.4	62.5	m

*Public institutions only.
Germany: data for special classes are included in those given for special schools.
Ireland: data are missing for Category 11 (severely and profoundly mentally handicapped) in special schools.
Czech Republic: data are missing for Category 1 (mentally retarded) in regular classes i.e. They refer to Category 6 (multiple handicaps) only.
Turkey: data refer only to compulsory school period (ISCED 1).

Discussion

As noted the regularity in this gender data is noteworthy but again remains difficult to interpret. The greater fragility of boys at birth might account for some of the variance as revealed in the data on individual categories in Tables 6.7, 6.8 and 6.9. However, the phenomenon is not restricted to students with impairments and why boys should receive such consistent additional resources remains obscure. These differences could be seen as responses to variations in the ways males and females express dissatisfaction with the system and as reflecting policies of positive discrimination. Whether positive discrimination for boys is in fact inequitable remains unresolved and requires further analysis.

Student/Staff ratios

Teaching and other staff are some of the most important resources made available to support the education of students with special educational needs. While it was felt to be highly desirable to collect data about support staff of various kinds, the pilot work on the development of the data collection instrument (discussed in Chapter 2) established that this information was rarely available at national level. While there is somewhat greater availability of data on teachers themselves it appears at the present time to be largely limited to the situation in special schools. Chart 6.4 gives an analysis of student/teacher ratios in these schools, split where data are available into primary and lower secondary stages of education.

Chart 6.4. **Student/teacher ratios in special schools**

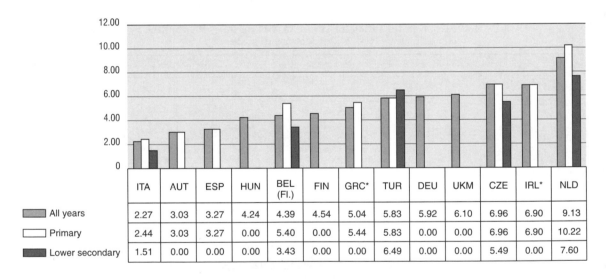

	ITA	AUT	ESP	HUN	BEL (Fl.)	FIN	GRC*	TUR	DEU	UKM	CZE	IRL*	NLD
All years	2.27	3.03	3.27	4.24	4.39	4.54	5.04	5.83	5.92	6.10	6.96	6.90	9.13
Primary	2.44	3.03	3.27	0.00	5.40	0.00	5.44	5.83	0.00	0.00	6.96	6.90	10.22
Lower secondary	1.51	0.00	0.00	0.00	3.43	0.00	0.00	6.49	0.00	0.00	5.49	0.00	7.60

*Public institutions only.
Belgium (Flemish Community): includes upper secondary students (ISCED 3).

These ratios, ranging from 2.27 to 9.13 for all years of schooling are clearly highly favourable compared to those in regular education which range from 10.8 (Italy) to 28.3 (Luxembourg) across primary and lower secondary levels (OECD, 1998). It is interesting to note that for the five countries for which comparative primary and lower secondary data are available, four show ratios in lower secondary which are less than that in primary, and one the reverse.

Table 6.10 provides student/teacher ratios in special schools for those individual national categories for which data are available. Some trends are discernible with, for example ratios for visual impairment categories tending to be lower than those for hearing impairment categories (although Hungary shows a small difference in the reverse direction). Both these categories tend to have lower student/teacher ratios than the mental impairment categories; particularly those labelled as relating to milder degrees of disability.

Age distribution of students with special educational needs

About one half of the countries from which usable quantitative data were obtained were able to provide a breakdown by age of students with special educational needs. The data are based on statistics provided in Table 6 of Annex 3. As with other aspects of the exercise, more complete data were obtained for special schools, with weaker data sets relating to special classes, and with few countries being able to provide these data for students working in fully integrated settings. Charts 6.5A to 6.5I inclusive present distributions for special schools, incorporating a gender split where data are available. Charts 6.6A and 6.6B give corresponding data for special classes.

Table 6.10. **Student/teacher ratios in special schools for individual national categories**

	National category	Category label	Students	Staff FTE	Student/ staff ratio
Greece*	1	Blind	54	18	3
	2	Deaf/hearing impaired	390	106	3.68
	3	Physically handicapped	289	76	3.8
	4	Mentally retarded	2536	448	5.66
Hungary	3	Visual disabilities	507	132	3.84
	4	Hearing disabilities	1145	339	3.38
	5	Motoric disabilities	372	184	2.02
	6	Speech disabilities	356	77	4.62
Ireland*	1	Visually impaired	91	19	4.79
	2	Hearing impaired	388	70	5.54
	3	Mild mental handicap	3182	260	12.24
	4	Moderate mental handicap	1779	250	7.12
	7	Physically handicapped	541	51	10.61
	9	Specific learning disability	248	23	10.78
	12	Multiple handicapped	38	6	6.33
	10**	Children of travelling families	207	18	11.5
	13**	Young offenders	254	47	5.4
Netherlands	2	Hard of hearing	2156	349.6	6.17
	5	Physically handicapped motor impairment	2526	412.8	6.12
	6	Other health impairments	4066	486	8.37
	7	Learning disabilities	39352	3802.3	10.35
	8	Profound mental handicap - severe learning disabilities	10520	1239.5	8.49
	9	Deviant behaviour	7714	1264.4	6.10
	10	Children with SEN/learning disabilities	40480	3625.4	11.17
	11	Chronic conditions requiring paedological institutes	1465	203.6	7.20
	12	Multiple handicapped	3946	912.6	4.32
Turkey	1	Visually impaired	563	128	4.4
	2	Hearing impaired	4665	733	6.36
	3	Orthopaedically handicapped	90	23	3.91
	4	Educable mentally handicapped	332	41	8.1
	5	Trainable mentally handicapped	1705	312	5.46
	8	Chronically ill	149	50	2.98

*Public institutions only.
** Placed in cross-national Category C.
All others placed in cross-national Category A.
FTE: full-time equivalent.

Chart 6.5. **Age distribution in special schools**

Number of students in that age group

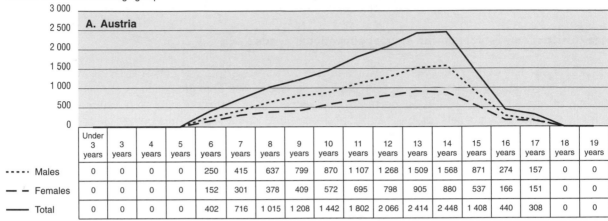

	Under 3 years	3 years	4 years	5 years	6 years	7 years	8 years	9 years	10 years	11 years	12 years	13 years	14 years	15 years	16 years	17 years	18 years	19 years
Males	0	0	0	0	250	415	637	799	870	1 107	1 268	1 509	1 568	871	274	157	0	0
Females	0	0	0	0	152	301	378	409	572	695	798	905	880	537	166	151	0	0
Total	0	0	0	0	402	716	1 015	1 208	1 442	1 802	2 066	2 414	2 448	1 408	440	308	0	0

Age group

Number of students in that age group

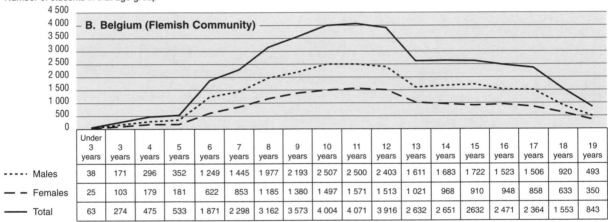

	Under 3 years	3 years	4 years	5 years	6 years	7 years	8 years	9 years	10 years	11 years	12 years	13 years	14 years	15 years	16 years	17 years	18 years	19 years
Males	38	171	296	352	1 249	1 445	1 977	2 193	2 507	2 500	2 403	1 611	1 683	1 722	1 523	1 506	920	493
Females	25	103	179	181	622	853	1 185	1 380	1 497	1 571	1 513	1 021	968	910	948	858	633	350
Total	63	274	475	533	1 871	2 298	3 162	3 573	4 004	4 071	3 916	2 632	2 651	2632	2 471	2 364	1 553	843

Age group

Number of students in that age group

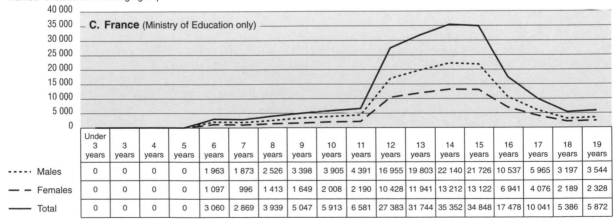

	Under 3 years	3 years	4 years	5 years	6 years	7 years	8 years	9 years	10 years	11 years	12 years	13 years	14 years	15 years	16 years	17 years	18 years	19 years
Males	0	0	0	0	1 963	1 873	2 526	3 398	3 905	4 391	16 955	19 803	22 140	21 726	10 537	5 965	3 197	3 544
Females	0	0	0	0	1 097	996	1 413	1 649	2 008	2 190	10 428	11 941	13 212	13 122	6 941	4 076	2 189	2 328
Total	0	0	0	0	3 060	2 869	3 939	5 047	5 913	6 581	27 383	31 744	35 352	34 848	17 478	10 041	5 386	5 872

Age group

Chart 6.5. **Age distribution in special schools** *(cont.)*

Number of students in that age group

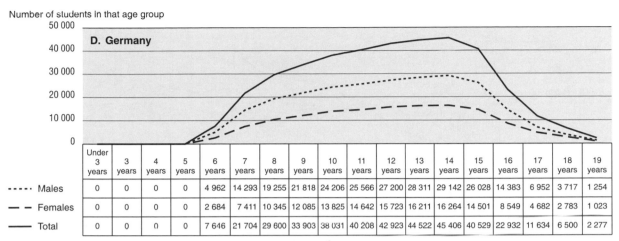

D. Germany

	Under 3 years	3 years	4 years	5 years	6 years	7 years	8 years	9 years	10 years	11 years	12 years	13 years	14 years	15 years	16 years	17 years	18 years	19 years
----- Males	0	0	0	0	4 962	14 293	19 255	21 818	24 206	25 566	27 200	28 311	29 142	26 028	14 383	6 952	3 717	1 254
– – Females	0	0	0	0	2 684	7 411	10 345	12 085	13 825	14 642	15 723	16 211	16 264	14 501	8 549	4 682	2 783	1 023
—— Total	0	0	0	0	7 646	21 704	29 600	33 903	38 031	40 208	42 923	44 522	45 406	40 529	22 932	11 634	6 500	2 277

Age group

Number of students in that age group

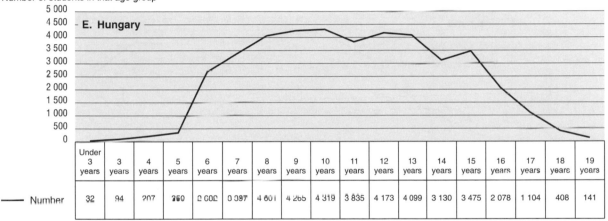

E. Hungary

	Under 3 years	3 years	4 years	5 years	6 years	7 years	8 years	9 years	10 years	11 years	12 years	13 years	14 years	15 years	16 years	17 years	18 years	19 years
—— Number	32	94	207	350	2 000	3 097	4 601	4 265	4 319	3 835	4 173	4 099	3 130	3 475	2 078	1 104	408	141

Age group

Number of students in that age group

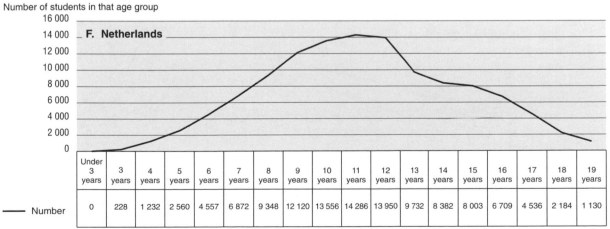

F. Netherlands

	Under 3 years	3 years	4 years	5 years	6 years	7 years	8 years	9 years	10 years	11 years	12 years	13 years	14 years	15 years	16 years	17 years	18 years	19 years
—— Number	0	228	1 232	2 560	4 557	6 872	9 348	12 120	13 556	14 286	13 950	9 732	8 382	8 003	6 709	4 536	2 184	1 130

Age group

Chart 6.5. **Age distribution in special schools** *(cont.)*

Number of students in that age group

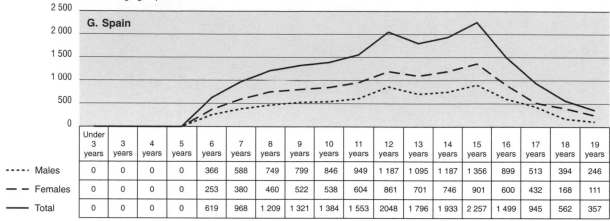

G. Spain

	Under 3 years	3 years	4 years	5 years	6 years	7 years	8 years	9 years	10 years	11 years	12 years	13 years	14 years	15 years	16 years	17 years	18 years	19 years
····· Males	0	0	0	0	366	588	749	799	846	949	1 187	1 095	1 187	1 356	899	513	394	246
– – Females	0	0	0	0	253	380	460	522	538	604	861	701	746	901	600	432	168	111
—— Total	0	0	0	0	619	968	1 209	1 321	1 384	1 553	2048	1 796	1 933	2 257	1 499	945	562	357

Age group

Number of students in that age group

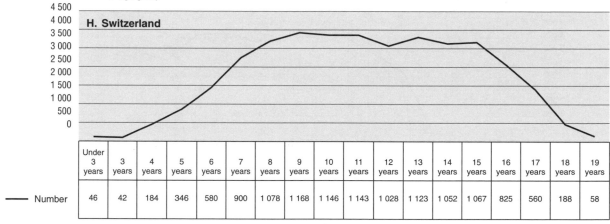

H. Switzerland

	Under 3 years	3 years	4 years	5 years	6 years	7 years	8 years	9 years	10 years	11 years	12 years	13 years	14 years	15 years	16 years	17 years	18 years	19 years
—— Number	46	42	184	346	580	900	1 078	1 168	1 146	1 143	1 028	1 123	1 052	1 067	825	560	188	58

Age group

Number of students in that age group

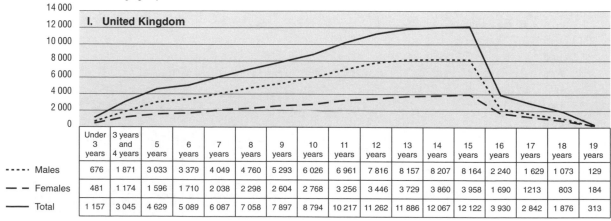

I. United Kingdom

	Under 3 years	3 years and 4 years	5 years	6 years	7 years	8 years	9 years	10 years	11 years	12 years	13 years	14 years	15 years	16 years	17 years	18 years	19 years
····· Males	676	1 871	3 033	3 379	4 049	4 760	5 293	6 026	6 961	7 816	8 157	8 207	8 164	2 240	1 629	1 073	129
– – Females	481	1 174	1 596	1 710	2 038	2 298	2 604	2 768	3 256	3 446	3 729	3 860	3 958	1 690	1213	803	184
—— Total	1 157	3 045	4 629	5 089	6 087	7 058	7 897	8 794	10 217	11 262	11 886	12 067	12 122	3 930	2 842	1 876	313

Age group

Chart 6.6.   **Age distribution in special classes**

Number of students in that age group

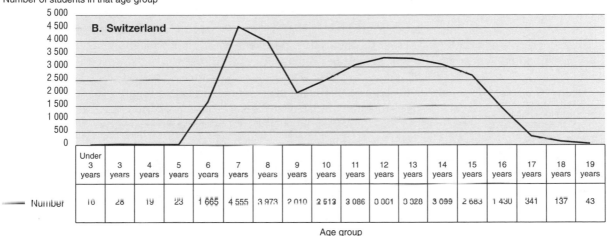

	Under 3 years	3 years	4 years	5 years	6 years	7 years	8 years	9 years	10 years	11 years	12 years	13 years	14 years	15 years	16 years	17 years	18 years	19 years
- - - - Males	0	0	0	0	11	39	62	90	131	141	155	173	215	180	48	12	0	0
— — Females	0	0	0	0	9	18	46	42	63	72	95	87	133	128	30	8	0	0
—— Total	0	0	0	0	20	57	108	132	194	213	250	260	348	308	78	20	0	0

Age group

Number of students in that age group

	Under 3 years	3 years	4 years	5 years	6 years	7 years	8 years	9 years	10 years	11 years	12 years	13 years	14 years	15 years	16 years	17 years	18 years	19 years
—— Number	10	28	19	23	1 665	4 555	3 973	2 010	2 513	3 086	3 001	3 328	3 099	2 683	1 430	341	137	43

Age group

Note: The unusual peak at seven years is caused by children who attend a special class for two years and are then integrated into second grade regular classes.

It is again noteworthy that the 60% rule (*i.e.* students with special needs split roughly in the ratio of three males to two females, irrespective of the particular breakdown used) discussed above in relation to the section on gender breakdowns, is strongly in evidence in these age breakdowns.

Discussion

For special schools, in general terms, the graphs show a linear increase in numbers with age starting at 3-5 and finishing at 10-15 according to country. France is the exception, with a relatively flat curve from 5-11 and a five fold increase in numbers at the transition from primary to secondary school at age 11.

After the graph peaks there is frequently a rapid decline as students leave the system, although Belgium (Flemish Community) and the Netherlands are notable exceptions where a decline occurs between the ages of 12 and 13. These changes would appear to reflect different policies and practices in the various countries.

Few countries were able to provide information on age distributions in special classes.

ISCED levels

Countries were also asked to report data on national categories broken down by ISECD levels 0, 1, 2, and 3 which covers pre-school, primary, lower secondary and upper secondary phases of education. The number of countries able to report data at ISCED levels 1 and 3 were slightly fewer than for levels 1 and 2. For example, in special schools, typically 10–12 countries out of 20 reported data for 1 and 2 with 7 to 9 able to do so for 0 and 3. The quantity of data was lower in other settings, with about one-quarter of countries reporting ISCED level data for levels 0 and 3 compared with a third to a half for 1 and 2.

Thus some data is available for a more complete analysis but extra effort will need to be made to improve this component of the database.

Resourcing

Data in the form of relative resourcing for students with special educational needs was requested in Table 7 (see Annex 3) but was virtually non-existent. Hungary, the Czech Republic and the Netherlands were able to provide partial data. For example, in the Czech Republic primary phase students with special needs (all national categories falling within the resources definition) are resourced in financial terms at 208% in special schools, 129% in special classes and 117% in regular classes of the resourcing provided for "regular" students. Corresponding figures at lower secondary level are 195%, 125% and 140%. In Hungary the figures are 200% at primary level and 180% at lower secondary, irrespective of location of education. In the Netherlands the corresponding figures are 300% at primary and 200% at lower secondary.

Hungary also provides data on the relative resourcing in personnel terms. At primary level relative resourcing of teachers is 220% (special needs students compared to "regular" students), of other professionals is 150% and of indirect support staff is also 150%. Corresponding figures at lower secondary level are 220%, 130% and 130%.

There is a little further data from other countries but this is difficult to interpret within the terms of the table.

It is clear that an alternative methodology will have to be pursued if worthwhile data on this crucially important aspect of resourcing are to be obtained.

Chapter 7

DISCUSSION AND CONCLUSIONS

Students with disabilities, learning or behaviour difficulties or disadvantages, represent a large and heterogeneous set of individuals who have in common the likelihood that they will be relatively unsuccessful in school unless additional effort is made to help them to access the curriculum and learn effectively. Among the countries of the OECD these students are conceptualised differently and given different labels. The more traditional approach is to identify students with disabilities through their main medical condition such as the visually impaired, the deaf, etc., and group these students together in specially adapted educational establishments. Those with learning difficulties and disadvantages, with less clear aetiologies have usually stayed in regular schools and in one way or another have been provided with extra help *e.g.* remedial education.

A different approach is to attack the problem from the point of view of the educational adaptations that have to be made to meet the educational needs of students who have difficulty with learning no matter what the apparent aetiology. The more formal concept of special educational needs is used to describe this approach, which makes it up to the school to adapt itself to meet the challenges presented by these needs. Such an approach underpins the inclusion movement (*e.g.* OECD, 1999a).

In practice, in OECD countries, these two frameworks are working in parallel with different aspects emphasised in different countries. As a consequence, there is little consistency in any of the terminology in use, although in general terms, as revealed in Chapter 3, there is a move towards the latter more inclusive framework. This lack of consistency applies as much, it seems, to definitions, as revealed in Table 3.2, as it does to the concept of special education, which in some countries is applied only to students with disabilities, while in others it covers those with disabilities, difficulties, disadvantages and in some the gifted.

Providing some comparative coherence to this highly complex field, which for want of a better term has been referred to in the monograph by using the very broad definition of "special education", through the gathering of statistics and the identification of education policy relevant indicators, is the task that was set. A task given extra impetus by the lack of relevant educational indicators in the general UOE effort in this area, the change to the definition of special education in ISCED-97 (which switches emphasis from the disability category model to the more open special educational needs approach) and a growing concern world wide about equity and inclusion issues.

Chapter 4 provides an analysis based on a more traditional approach, and the comparative difficulties are self-evident. The analysis nevertheless reveals the considerable differences among countries not only in the numbers of students apparently experiencing disabling conditions but also in the location of their education.

The method used to tackle these challenges has been set out in the previous chapters and will not be repeated here. But a few words are in order commenting on the general effectiveness of the approach used. A resources model was used to identify the maximum number of students who receive additional help and to assist in overcoming the variations in the use of terms in Member countries. It is fair to conclude that this approach achieved the second of these goals. However, limitation on data availability (including situations where resources were provided from sources other than education) mean that it is not possible to provide totally accurate figures for the total number of students involved in all cases. As Chapter 5 shows, for some countries data was included when this definition was used which is likely to have been excluded had the term "special education" been used. Thus within the limits of the availability of data (which are in fact considerable) we can have some confidence that the very general figures, *e.g.* as presented in Chart 5.1, show a more accurate picture than heretofore.

The resources model provides global figures which it is then necessary to break down on the basis of some other criteria which could in principle allow for international comparisons, and the cross-national classifications of A, B and C as defined in Chapter 1 have been developed for this purpose. Countries were asked to put their own national categories into these three bands and the result is presented in Table 3.2. This table provides an extremely useful descriptive classification which helps considerably in understanding elements of the thinking lying behind national systems in terms of the causation of problems included under the broad heading of special education. As can be seen from Table 3.2 this exercise was also completed successfully and with some consistency, although more work is required to improve this framework.

The data derived from this method did, however, vary substantially as Chapters 5 and 6 show. The data for Category A was relatively good while those from B and C relatively poor. This latter problem substantially limits any analysis that might be made and a major effort to improve data quality for these categories will be made in the on-going phase of work. Chapter 5 shows that comparisons for Category A reveal much less variability than for disability categories taken separately, or for any of the other approaches attempted in this chapter, and increase confidence that the differences are real and not an artefact. If this is so, this variation raises the question of what underlies it. Data of this sort, cannot of course answer this question, but it is likely that the differences reflect a complex effect of factors such as medical care, educational policy and practices. The large differences revealed in the location of education for individual categories (whether in regular classes, special classes or special schools), also shown in Chapter 4, implicates the last two factors.

The numbers of students receiving additional resources because of disadvantage, as reported under Category "C", show substantial variation among countries (see Charts 5.13 and 5.14). An explanation of these differences requires further research since factors underlying disadvantage such as poverty and immigration levels vary substantially among countries. Although on face value it would appear that some countries are more generous in their provision for disadvantage, again this conclusion requires further work since countries also vary both in the basic levels of educational funding and in the sources of funding, *e.g.* from different ministries. Furthermore, it remains to be seen what links may exist between the extent of the additional provision made and educational and social outcomes.

The data presented in Chapter 6 on numbers and sizes of special schools and special classes show in different ways variations among countries in terms of provision made. It is clear that some countries maintain a very substantial special school sector whilst others do not. Data on the proportion of regular classes with special needs students was limited, but data from Italy gives some indication of the implications of integration. In Italy, 28.7% of primary classes and 37.7% of secondary classes contain a student placed in cross-national Category "A". The implications of this outcome are self-evident for the training of teachers and others who work in integrated schools and the finding emphasises the importance of appropriate training for successful integration.

One of the most surprising findings to emerge was the consistent appearance of a gender effect. In most countries supplying this breakdown, and across all cross-national categories an approximate 60:40 ratio appeared of males to females in special education systems. This robust finding is not easy to interpret, but its ubiquity makes it tempting to suggest that it reflects a systematic difference in the extent to which males and females are perceived to have special educational needs.

Because of the resources definition used in this study it seems to be clear that males are using more of the available resources than females. This may be interpreted as a positive discrimination in favour of males who are considered to be generally more at risk than females in current education and social systems. This remains another area where further research is needed to clarify the situation.

The data on student/staff ratios reveal substantial variations among countries and there are obvious financial implications of these large differences. And again there may be training implications.

The data on age distributions also show considerable between country variation which again would seem to reflect different policies and practices relating to identification and decision-making strategies in place in different countries in their responses to students who present difficulties.

Finally in summary, this study brings together data pertaining to students with disabilities, learning or behaviour difficulties and disadvantages in participating countries of the OECD. Based on additional resources supplied, and a cross-national classification system, it attempts to provide a unifying framework to allow for improved international comparisons of educational provision for this large group of students. A start has been made, but there is still a long way to go in terms of both refining the system and improving data quality. When this is achieved the groundwork will have been laid for extending the analyses into a comparison of outcomes, and even opening the possibility of linking inputs to outputs. These are the challenges for the coming years.

The data reveal large variations among countries in the number and gender of students registered in educational statistics with special educational needs, the extent and type of provision made, the resources available, and the places where these students are being educated; in brief, in the way the system works to support students in difficulty. The consistent gender differences identified among countries raises important policy issues relating to the identification and treatment of males and females. Whether the system is operating equitably, in terms of the assessment of students with special needs and the associated increased resources needs careful consideration. This is of especial significance, for instance, in view of the negative implications, in terms of future prospects, of being educated in special schools. For a fuller discussion of these issues, see Evans (2000).

The study is continuing and will be focusing on improving data quality and expanding the database, where possible to cover pre-school, upper secondary and post-school periods including further and higher education. Work measuring a range of outcomes in both academic and non-academic areas will also be carried out over the coming years.

REFERENCES

EURYDICE (1996), *Information Dossiers on the Structures of the Education Systems in the European Union and the EFTA Countries 1996: The Netherlands* (Revised edition, December 1996).

EVANS, P. (2000), *Developing Equity Indicators based on Additional Resources supplied for Disabled and Disadvantaged Students*, OECD, Paris, in press.

OECD (1995), *Integrating Students with Special Needs into Mainstream Schools*, Paris.

OECD (1998), *Education at a Glance – OECD Indicators*, Paris.

OECD (1999a), *Inclusive Education at Work: Including Students with Disabilities into Mainstream Schools*, Paris.

OECD (1999b), *Classifying Educational Programmes – Manual for ISCED-97 Implementation in OECD Countries*, 1999 Edition, Paris.

OECD (2000), *Education at a Glance – OECD indicators*, Paris.

UNESCO (1997), *International Standard Classification of Education – ISCED*, Paris.

QUESTIONNAIRE

Please refer to the "Notes on Questionnaire" below for general guidance in completing the questionnaire, and for notes on specific questions.

> If possible please type the response to all questions. If this is not possible please complete legibly, preferably using CAPITAL LETTERS.

Q1. Who is responsible for ensuring the completion of the Questionnaire and Data Collection Tables?

Please give details in the box below:

> Name:
>
> Address:
>
> Telephone number:
>
> Fax number:
>
> e-mail address:

Q2. What DEFINITION of special educational needs is currently used in collecting educational statistics in your educational system?

Please provide the definition in the box below:

Q3. Do you use CATEGORIES of special educational needs in collecting data about your educational system?

Yes/No

> If **No**, please **Skip to Q7**

If **Yes**, please list the names of the categories and provide the full definition which you use for the category.

Please note that inclusion of a category here should *be in terms of your own definition of special educational needs* as given in answer to Q2 above and NOT *in terms of the "resources" definition* (unless this is the definition of special educational needs which you use).

Please indicate in the right-hand column whether a category also falls within the "resources" definition (i.e. do you provide additional resources to support students in this category). [please refer to the operational definitions in Chapter 1]

There is provision for up to fifteen categories below. IF more than fifteen categories are used for data collection in your system please make photocopies of the following page(s), renumber and append.

Category 1

Name of category	Does category fall within "resources" definition?
Definition of category	Yes/No

Category 2-20, etc.

Q4. Are there any CATEGORIES of students, currently used for data collection in your educational system, which fall within the "resources" definition BUT WHICH YOU DO NOT CONSIDER TO FALL WITHIN YOUR DEFINITION OF SPECIAL NEEDS?

Yes/No

If **Yes** please list the names of the categories and provide the full definition which you use for the category.

There is provision for up to five such categories below. IF more than five categories please make photocopies of the following page(s), renumber and append.

Category 4.1 (falling within "resources" definition but NOT considered to fall within your special needs definition)

Name of category
Definition of category

Category 4.2-4.5, etc.

Q5. Can you specify whether SUBSTANTIAL or MINIMAL ADDITIONAL RESOURCES are made available to support students within the categories given in answer to Q3 and Q4?

Yes/No

If **Yes** please provide information **for each of the above categories to which a "Yes" answer was given to "Does category fall within resources definition?" in answer to Q3, and also any categories included in answer to Q4.**

Add further rows if necessary to accommodate additional categories

Number of category (as in Q3 and Q4)	Name of category	Substantial or minimal (tick appropriate column)	

Q6. Where do you consider that the categories for which data are available within your system (as specified in response to Q3 and Q4) fit within the cross-national categorisation?

> **PLEASE RECORD AS THE ANSWER TO THIS QUESTION THE RESULTS OF THE** "Exercise on Relationship between Categories in Different National Systems and Cross-National Categorisation" (see Annex 1 of the Instrument). **IF IT IS NOT POSSIBLE TO CARRY OUT THE EXERCISE IN ANNEX 1 PLEASE SIMPLY INDICATE BY "X" A CHOICE OF A, B, OR C FOR EACH CATEGORY.**

Note that ALL categories entered in response to Q3 should be used here; *i.e.* **both those considered to fall within the resource definition and those considered not to, as well as ALL categories entered in response to Q4.**

Please insert in the table the **NUMBER of independent judges** placing each category into each column (*i.e.* the number considering a category to fit into cross-national category A, B or C. Record separately any use of "1" or "2" indicating a split vote).

Please also indicate for each category the **CONSENSUS view** by placing a cross (**x**) in the appropriate box.

An example of the required coding is presented as category "0"– it indicates that two judges chose "B"; seven chose "C"; one had a split vote between those two categories putting "C" first and "B" second; and that the consensus was "C."

Category as given in answer to Q3 and Q4 (please repeat number and label for category) ABC	A	B	C
0. Example of coding	0	2+1 "2"	7+1 "1" **X**

PLEASE SKIP TO Q8

THIS QUESTION IS ONLY FOR THOSE WHO ANSWERED "NO" TO Q3 (*i.e.* "Do you use CATEGORIES of special educational needs in collecting data about your educational system?")

Q7. How are planning decisions made to ensure that students with special educational needs receive appropriate additional resources?

Please give details in the box below, or attach relevant statements or publications. Information about the basis for any such decisions (*e.g.* sample surveys) and of the bases for estimations of incidence or prevalence of different special educational needs (*e.g.* in deriving funding formulae) would be appreciated

[empty box]

Q8. Is there specific coverage of special educational needs in the LEGISLATIVE FRAMEWORK in place in your country?

Yes/No

If **Yes**, please append details of the relevant legislation in the box below and add any comments on the way that this framework influences special needs provision

[empty box]

Q9. Can you identify characteristics of YOUR educational system which you believe to act as FACILITATORS OF EQUITY AND INCLUSIVE EDUCATION?

Yes/No

If **Yes**, please give details in the box below.

[empty box]

Q10. Can you identify characteristics of YOUR educational system which you believe to act as BARRIERS TO EQUITY AND INCLUSIVE EDUCATION?

Yes/No

If **Yes,** please give details in the box below.

[empty box]

NOTES ON QUESTIONNAIRE

Question 1

This question asks for details of the person taking responsibility for completion of the questionnaire and data collection tables. This is so that in the event of any queries a contact person is available.

Question 2

For the purpose of this question give the definition of special educational needs which is used for collecting educational statistics in your system. If you have a definition but it is NOT used for statistical purposes please indicate this, and also give the definition. Note that, while the term "special educational needs" is used in the instrument, it is to be regarded as referring to the same general area as "special needs", "special education", and "special needs education".

Question 3

This question asks for the categories of special educational needs used for collecting educational statistics in your system.

You are also asked to indicate whether or not you consider that these categories fall within the "resources" definition of special educational needs. To help in making this decision recall that the definition is:

> Those with special educational needs are defined by the additional public and/or private resources provided to support their education.

And that use of this definition in a consistent manner calls for agreement about the term ADDITIONAL and an appreciation of the various kinds of possible RESOURCES PROVIDED which should be considered.

> "Additional resources" are those made available over and above the resources generally available where no consideration is given to needs of students likely to have particular difficulties in accessing the regular curriculum [the term "student" is used throughout this instrument. It is to be regarded as synonymous with "pupil" or "(school) child"].

Resources can be of many different kinds. Examples are:

> PERSONNEL RESOURCES. These include a more favourable teacher/student ratio than in a regular classroom where no allowance is being made for students with special needs; additional teachers, assistants or any other personnel (for some or all of the time); training programmes for teachers and others which equip them for work in special needs education.

> MATERIAL RESOURCES. These include aids or supports of various types (*e.g.* hearing aid); modifications or adaptations to classroom; specialised teaching materials

OECD 2000

FINANCIAL RESOURCES. These include funding formulae which are more favourable to those with special needs (including classes where it is known or assumed that there are students with special needs); systems where money is set aside for special educational needs within the regular budget allocation; payments made in support of special needs education; and the costs of personnel and material resources.

The key question is whether these resources are made available to "support their education" and are provided when students have "particular difficulties in accessing the regular curriculum". Any resources which meet these criteria should be considered.

As it is possible to argue that virtually any resource could be used to "support education" in some sense, the directness of the link to education should be taken into account. For example:

a) the provision of a hearing aid for partially hearing students may be considered to be of direct relevance to their education (note that under the "resources" type of definition the special educational need does not disappear when the aid is provided).

b) modification of the curriculum or of its delivery could fall under the definition if it is more resource-intensive (*e.g.* calls for assistance or lower student-teacher ratio) and is to support the education of students who have difficulties in accessing the regular curriculum.

c) provision of transport to a residential facility or relatively distant school or unit, which may be a resource in excess of that provided for students with no particular difficulties in accessing the regular curriculum, may provide direct support for the education of students required to attend the distant facility; or for students from a disadvantaged background.

d) giving food or clothing to children in poverty provides a more difficult case. However, it might be thought that a programme with educational aims which targeted such needs would fall within the definition.

e) A road-building or disease eradication programme, while it might be demonstrated to have educational consequences, might be seen as outside any reasonable interpretation of direct support to education.

Question 4

This question asks for details of any categories of students, which are used for data collection in your system, and which you consider to fall within the "resources" definition, *but are not regarded as falling within your own definition of special educational needs*. For example:

a) additional resources may be provided for students from a disadvantaged background but this may not fall within the national definition of special educational needs.

b) you may collect data on the category "gifted children" and also provide additional resources to students so categorised but not consider this to fall within your definition of special educational needs.

c) you may collect data on the category "immigrant children" and also provide additional resources to students so categorised to support learning their mother tongue, but not consider this to fall within your definition of special educational needs.

In each of these examples it is of course possible that they would fall within your definition of special needs.

The answers to questions 3 and 4, which form the basis for entries to the data collection tables, taken together permit analysis in terms of national categories of special educational need *and* in terms of the resources definition. It will also be possible compare different countries interpretation of special educational needs and of the resources definition.

Question 5

For the purposes of this question, *substantial* should be taken as referring to a situation where clear and obvious additional resources of some kind, or kinds, are provided (*e.g.* the student/teacher ratio is significantly smaller than that of a regular classroom where no allowance is made for students with special educational needs; or where, in proportional terms, per capita funding is significantly higher than the norm for regular education).

Minimal should be taken to refer to a situation where some identifiable additional resources of some kind, or kinds, are provided but these are small in proportional terms, being unlikely to exceed the variability of resource found in regular classrooms where no allowance is made for students with special educational needs.

It is appreciated that there may be a strong element of subjective judgement in making these decisions about resources and any comments which would assist in interpreting the response are welcomed.

Question 6

The study has adopted a simple scheme attempting to assist cross-national comparisons of categories of special educational needs. It is referred to as the *cross-national categorisation of special educational needs*. This is, in part, to link to the previously used categories based on disability in the interest of continuity and of interpretation of data gathered under a resource-based model.

In this categorisation there are *three categories* referred to as **A, B** and **C** (Note: pilot work established that any short label attached to these categories was liable to be differentially interpreted in different countries).

Definition of Category A

Refers to educational needs of students where there is substantial normative agreement – such as blind and partially sighted, deaf and partially hearing, severe and profound mental handicap, multiple handicaps. Conditions which affect students from all social classes and occupations. Typically adequate measuring instruments and agreed criteria are available. Typically considered in medical terms to be organic disorders attributable to organic pathologies (*e.g.* in relation to sensory, motor or neurological defects).

Definition of Category B

Refers to educational needs of students who have difficulties in learning which do not appear to be directly or primarily attributable to factors which would lead to categorisation as A or C.

Definition of Category C

Refers to educational needs of students which are considered to arise primarily from socio-economic, cultural and/or linguistic factors. There is some form of disadvantaged or atypical background for which education seeks to compensate

This question is linked to the "Exercise on Relationship Between Categories in Different National Systems and Cross-National Categorisation" which forms Annex 1 of the instrument. This exercise calls for the recruitment of ten persons with a good knowledge of the system of education in your country as it relates to those with special educational needs. They are asked to use their knowledge and judgement in deciding into which of these three categories each of your national categories of special educational need is best placed. In this way it may be possible to make cross-national comparisons with increased reliability and validity and analyse possible anomalies, while still retaining information in terms of national categories.

It will be noted that category B is effectively a residual category; *i.e.* that the decision called for is whether a national category is A or C; if neither it is B. In this way the categorisation is forced to be exhaustive, *i.e.* all national categories must fall into A, B or C. Further examples of the use of the categories have been avoided at this stage but it is anticipated that the definitions may be refined in the light of the results obtained from this version of the instrument.

The strategy of asking for several persons to carry out this exercise was indicated because pilot work in some countries showed areas of disagreement on allocation of national categories between individuals. If it is not possible to perform the exercise the person responsible for the completion of the questionnaire should ensure that an allocation of the national categories to A, B or C is carried out by someone familiar with special educational needs and the national categories.

A response to this question is crucial for the analysis and interpretation of the data tables.

Question 7

It is recognised that some countries, particularly where there is a commitment to integration and to such notions as "schools for all" may not consider it appropriate to collect statistics on the basis of categories of special educational needs.

The question invites exposition of how educational planning in this field is carried out in the absence of these statistics.

Question 8

National (and in some countries, regional) legislative framework relating to special educational needs provides useful contextual information which may assist in understanding and interpreting features of special educational needs provision.

Questions 9 and 10

There may be additional types of contextual information which assist in understanding and interpreting features of special educational needs provision. They either:

a) tend to have a positive influence on equity of treatment for, and the integration of, those with special educational needs into mainstream education (FACILITATORS) or

b) tend to have a negative influence on the equity of treatment for, and integration of, those with special educational needs into mainstream education (BARRIERS)

For example, certain types of funding formulae provide financial incentives for local authorities/municipalities or regions to place students in segregated settings. Other approaches where, effectively, a student with special educational needs carries funding with her or him may have an opposite effect.

The question invites information in this area which may help in understanding the statistical data provided in the data collection tables.

Annex 1

EXERCISE ON RELATIONSHIP BETWEEN CATEGORIES IN DIFFERENT NATIONAL SYSTEMS AND CROSS-NATIONAL CATEGORISATION

Instructions

This exercise is linked to question 6 of the Questionnaire. You are requested to carry out this exercise with **TEN** persons who have a good knowledge of the system of education in your country as it relates to those with special educational needs.

You may wish to use the pro-forma on the following page, having inserted the numbers and names of **ALL THE CATEGORIES ENTERED IN RESPONSE TO Q3 AND Q4 IN THE QUESTIONNAIRE**. Alternatively, and preferably, produce your own version (translated if appropriate) which incorporates these categories.

For the first phase respondents should complete the exercise **INDEPENDENTLY** though please feel free to clarify any aspect of the exercise with them.

After the results of this independent phase have been collected a **CONSENSUS VIEW** from the respondents should be sought through discussion for the allocation of each category used in your system to the cross-national categorisation.

The results should be entered as the response to Q6. Please also add any comments on the exercise.

EXERCISE ON RELATIONSHIP BETWEEN CATEGORIES OF SPECIAL EDUCATIONAL NEED IN DIFFERENT SYSTEMS AND A CROSS-NATIONAL CATEGORISATION

The Cross-National categorisation is **A, B** and **C**. The categories are defined as follows:

Category A

> Refers to educational needs of students where there is substantial normative agreement – such as blind and partially sighted, deaf and partially hearing, severe and profound mental handicap, multiple handicaps. Conditions which affect students from all social classes and occupations. Typically adequate measuring instruments and agreed criteria are available. Typically considered in medical terms to be organic disorders attributable to organic pathologies (*e.g.* in relation to sensory, motor or neurological defects).

Category B

> Refers to educational needs of students who have difficulties in learning which do not appear to be directly or primarily attributable to factors which would lead to categorisation as A or C.

Category C

> Refers to educational needs of students which are considered to arise primarily from socio-economic, cultural and/or linguistic factors. There is some form of disadvantaged or atypical background for which education seeks to compensate.

113

The table below lists the categories for which data are available in your system.

Please indicate by a tick in the appropriate box of the table where you consider each category to fit into the cross-national categorisation (*e.g.* if you use the term "blind" and consider that it falls within "A" tick that box.).

If you consider that one of your categories falls within more than one category in the system, indicate the category which it fits best by "1", the next best by "2".

National category	A	B	C

Annex 2

ISCED LEVELS OF EDUCATION

The descriptions below are taken from ISCED 1997 (151 EX/8 Annex II, March 1997, UNESCO) and are designed to assist in determining the level of educational programmes.

Level 0 – Pre-primary education

Principal characteristics

Programmes at Level 0 (pre-primary) defined as the initial stage of organised instruction are designed primarily to introduce very young children to a school-type environment, *i.e.* to provide a bridge between the home and a school based atmosphere. Upon completion of these programmes, children continue their education at Level 1 (primary education).

Classification criteria

For the definition of the beginning and the end of pre-primary education, *i.e.* the boundary between pre-primary education and childcare or between pre-primary and primary education, the following criteria are relevant:

Main criteria

- the educational properties of the programme;

- school or centre based;

- the minimum age of the children catered for; and

- the upper age limit of the children.

Subsidiary criterion

- the staff qualifications.

For a programme to be considered as pre-primary education, it has to be school-based or centre-based. These terms are used to distinguish activities in settings such as primary school, pre-schools and kindergartens from services provided in households or family settings.

Such programmes are designed for children aged at least three years. This age has been chosen since programmes destined for younger children do not normally satisfy the educational criteria in ISCED.

The upper age limit depends in each case on the typical age for entry into primary education.

Where appropriate, the requirement of pedagogical qualifications for the teaching staff can be a good proxy criterion for an educational programme in all those countries, in which such a requirement exists. It serves to distinguish pre-primary education from child-care for which para-medical or no qualifications are required.

Includes also:

This level includes organised instruction for children with special needs education. This education may be also provided in hospitals or in special schools or training centres. In this case no upper age limit can be specified.

Excludes:

Adult education.

Level 1 – Primary education or first stage of basic education

Principal characteristics

Programmes at Level 1 are normally designed on a unit or project basis to give students a sound basic education in reading, writing and mathematics along with an elementary understanding of other subjects such as history, geography, natural science, social science, art and music. In some cases religious instruction is featured.

The core at this level consists of education provided for children, the customary or legal age of entrance being not younger than five years or older than seven years. This level covers in principle six years of full-time schooling.

Throughout this level the programmes are organised in units or projects rather than by subjects. This is a principal characteristic differentiating programmes at this level in most countries from those at Level 2.

Classification criteria

For the definition of the boundary between education Levels 0 and 1 (pre-primary and primary education) the following criteria are relevant:

Main criterion

- the beginning of systematic studies characteristic of primary education, *e.g.* reading, writing and mathematics.

Subsidiary criteria

- entry into the nationally designated primary institutions or programmes, and the start of compulsory education where it exists.

Includes also:

In countries where primary education is part of "basic education", only the first stage should be included in Level 1. If "basic" education is not officially divided into stages, only the first six years should be classified as Level 1.

This level category also includes programmes suited to children with special educational needs.

Literacy programmes within or outside the school system which are similar in content to programmes in primary education for those considered too old to enter elementary schools are also, included at this level because they require no previous formal education.

Level 2 – Lower secondary or second stage of basic education

Principal characteristics

The contents of education at this stage are typically designed to complete the provision of basic education which began at ISCED Level 1. In many, if not most countries, the educational aim is to lay the foundation for lifelong learning and human development on which countries may expand, systematically, further educational opportunities. The programmes at this level are usually on a more subject oriented pattern using more specialised teachers and more often several teachers conducting classes in their field of specialisation. The full implementation of basic skills occurs at this level. The end of this level often coincides with the end of compulsory education where it exists.

Classification criteria

For the definition of this level, the following criteria are relevant:

Main criteria

- the beginning of subject presentation using more qualified teachers than for Level 1; and

- the full implementation of basic skills and foundation for lifelong learning.

Subsidiary criteria

- entry is after some six years of primary education,

- the end of this level is after some nine years of schooling since the beginning of primary education;

- the end of this level often coincides with the end of compulsory education in countries where this exists; and

- often, at the beginning of this level, several teachers start to conduct classes in their field of specialisation.

Complementary dimensions

Two complementary dimensions are needed to describe this level:

- the type of subsequent education or destination; and

- the programme orientation.

Type of subsequent education or destination

ISCED Level 2 programmes can be sub-classified according to the destination for which the programmes have been designated, resulting in the following distinction:

- ISCED 2A: programmes designed for direct access to Level 3 in a sequence which would ultimately lead to tertiary education, *i.e.* entrance to ISCED 3A or 3B;

- ISCED 2B: programmes designed for direct access to Level 3C;

- ISCED 2C: programmes primarily designed for direct access to the labour market at the end of this level (sometimes referred to as "terminal" programmes)

Programme orientation

This second complementary dimension subdivides the programmes into three categories:

General education

Education which is mainly designed to lead participants to a deeper understanding of a subject or group of subjects, especially, but not necessarily, with a view to preparing participants for further (additional) education at the same or a higher level. Successful completion of these programmes may or may not provide the participants with a labour-market relevant qualification at this level. These programmes are typically school-based. Programmes with a general orientation and not focusing on a particular specialisation should be classified in this category.

Pre-vocational and pre-technical education

Education which is mainly designed to introduce participants to the world of work and to prepare them for entry into vocational and technical education programmes. Successful completion of such programmes does not yet lead to a labour-market relevant vocational or technical qualification. For a programme to be considered as pre-vocational or pre-technical education, at least 25% of its content has to be vocational or technical. This minimum is necessary to ensure that the vocational subject or the technical subject is not only one among many others.

Vocational and technical education

Education which is mainly designed to lead participants to acquire the practical skills, know-how and understanding necessary for employment in a particular occupation or trade or class of occupations or trades. Successful completion of such programmes lead to a labour-market relevant vocational qualification recognised by the competent authority in the country in which it is obtained (*e.g.* Ministry of Education, employers associations, etc.).

Programmes in this category may be subdivided into two types:

- Those which are primarily theoretically oriented, and

- Those which are primarily practically oriented.

These three categories are also used for Levels 3 and 4.

Includes also:

In countries where primary education is part of "basic education", the second stage of basic education should be included in Level 2. If "basic education" is not officially divided into stages, the years after the sixth should be classified as Level 2.

This level includes special needs education programmes and all adult education which are similar in content to the education given at this level, *e.g.* the education which gives to adults the basic skills necessary for further learning.

Level 3: Upper secondary education

Principal characteristics

This level of education typically begins at the end of full-time compulsory education for those countries that have a system of compulsory education. More specialisation may be observed at this level than at ISCED Level 2 and often teachers need to be more qualified or specialised than for ISCED Level 2. The entrance age to this level is typically 15 or 16 years.

The educational programmes included at this level typically require the completion of some 9 years of full-time education (since the beginning of Level 1) for admission or a combination of education and vocational or technical experience and with as minimum entrance requirements the completion of Level 2 or demonstrable ability to handle programmes at this level.

Classification criteria

For the definition of this level, the following criteria are relevant:

Main criteria

- the typical entrance qualifications (some nine years of full-time education since the beginning of Level I); and

- the minimum entrance requirements (usually the completion of Level 2).

Complementary dimensions

Three dimensions are needed to sub-classify this level:

- type of subsequent education or destination;

- programme orientation; and

- cumulative theoretical duration in full time equivalent since the beginning of Level 3.

Type of subsequent education or destination

The first of these dimensions results in three distinct groupings:

- ISCED 3A: programmes at Level 3, designed to provide direct access to ISCED A;

- ISCED 3B: programmes at Level 3 designed to provide direct access to ISCED B;

- ISCED 3C: programmes at Level 3 not designed to lead directly to ISCED 5A or 5B. Therefore, these programmes lead directly to labour market, ISCED 4 programmes or other ISCED 3 programmes

Programme orientation

This second complementary dimension has the same categories as for Level 2:

- general education,

- pre-vocational and pre-technical education, and

- vocational and technical education.

Cumulative theoretical duration

This third dimension, the cumulative theoretical duration of the programme, in full-time equivalent, is calculated from the beginning of Level 3. This dimension is particularly useful for Level 3C programmes.

Includes also:

This level includes also special needs education programmes and adult education.

OECD 2000

Excludes:

Remedial programmes that are designed for participants who have pursued a programme at ISCED Level 2 but who have not obtained the objectives of ISCED Level 2 programmes (and which therefore cannot be regarded as equivalent in content to any of the ISCED 3 programmes described below) should not be classified at ISCED Level 3 but at ISCED Level 1 or 2 depending on the content of the programmes.

Annex 3

DATA TABLES

Table 1. **Information on years of compulsory schooling**

Reference date/period for data collection (month and year) _____ /1996

SYSTEM LEVEL INFORMATION	TYPE OF EDUCATIONAL PROGRAMME			
	SPECIAL EDUCATIONAL NEEDS PROGRAMMES IN SPECIAL SCHOOLS	SPECIAL EDUCATIONAL NEEDS PROGRAMMES IN SPECIAL CLASSES IN REGULAR SCHOOLS	SPECIAL EDUCATIONAL NEEDS PROGRAMMES IN REGULAR CLASSES IN REGULAR SCHOOLS	REGULAR EDUCATIONAL ROGRAMMES
	1	2	3	4
S1 Theoretical starting age of primary or basic school education				
S2 Theoretical ending age of primary or basic school education				
S3 Theoretical ending age of generally required school education				

Table 2. **Information on programmes for students in special schools classified according to national categories – All years of compulsory schooling**

STUDENTS IN NATIONAL CATEGORY 1. Name of category:

TYPE OF INSTITUTION	NUMBER OF INSTITUTIONS	TEACHING STAFF			STUDENTS ENROLLED		
		Total full-time and part-time	Full-time	Full-time equivalents	Total males and females	Males	Females
	1	2	3	4	5	6	7
				(3+4)	(6+7)		

PRIMARY OR BASIC SCHOOL EDUCATION

a1	Total public and private institutions	(a2+a3)					
a2	Public institutions						
a3	All private institutions	(a4+a5)					
a4	Government dependent private institutions						
a5	Independent private institutions						

SECONDARY EDUCATION

a6	Total public and private institutions	(a7+a8))					
a7	Public institutions						
a8	All private institutions	(a9+a10)					
a9	Government dependent private institutions						
a10	Independent private institutions						

ALL YEARS OF COMPULSORY SCHOOLING

a11	Total public and private institutions	(a12+a13)					
a12	Public institutions						
a13	All private institutions	(a14+a15)					
a14	Government dependent private institutions						
a15	Independent private institutions						

STUDENTS IN NATIONAL CATEGORY 2. Name of category:

Continuing up to category 20.

Table 2 (*continued*). **Students in special schools**

STUDENTS IN ALL NATIONAL CATEGORIES CONSIDERED TO FALL WITHIN "RESOURCES" DEFINITION COMBINED

NOTE: the categories to be added to form entries in this part of the table are given by your responses to Q3 and Q4

		NUMBER OF INSTITUTIONS	TEACHING STAFF			STUDENTS ENROLLED		
			Total full-time and part-time	Full-time	Full-time equivalents	Total males and females	Males	Females
		141	142	143	144	145	146	147
			(143+144)			(146+147)		

PRIMARY OR BASIC SCHOOL EDUCATION

	TYPE OF INSTITUTIONS								
a1	Total public and private institutions	(a2+a3)							
a2	Public institutions								
a3	All private institutions	(a4+a5)							
a4	Government dependent private institutions								
a5	Independent private institutions								

SECONDARY EDUCATION

a6	Total public and private institutions	(a7+a8))							
a7	Public institutions								
a8	All private institutions	(a9+a10)							
a9	Government dependent private institutions								
a10	Independent private institutions								

ALL YEARS OF COMPULSORY SCHOOLING

a11	Total public and private institutions	(a12+a13)							
a12	Public institutions								
a13	All private institutions	(a14+a15)							
a14	Government dependent private institutions								
a15	Independent private institutions								

Table 2 (*continued*). **Students in special schools**

STUDENTS IN ALL NATIONAL CATEGORIES OF SPECIAL EDUCATIONAL NEED COMBINED

NOTE: the categories to be added to from entries in this part of the table are given by your response to Q3

TYPE OF INSTITUTIONS	NUMBER OF INSTITUTIONS	TEACHING STAFF			STUDENTS ENROLLED		
		Total full-time and part-time	Full-time	Full-time equivalents	Total males and females	Males	Females
	148	149 (150+151)	150	151	152 (153+154)	153	154
PRIMARY OR BASIC SCHOOL EDUCATION							
a1 Total public and private institutions (a2+a3)							
a2 Public institutions							
a3 All private institutions (a4+a5)							
a4 Government dependent private institutions							
a5 Independent private institutions							
SECONDARY EDUCATION							
a6 Total public and private institutions (a7+a8)							
a7 Public institutions							
a8 All private institutions (a9+a10)							
a9 Government dependent private institutions							
a10 Independent private institutions							
ALL YEARS OF COMPULSORY SCHOOLING							
a11 Total public and private institutions (a12+a13)							
a12 Public institutions							
a13 All private institutions (a14+a15)							
a14 Government dependent private institutions							
a15 Independent private institutions							

Table 3. **Information on programmes for students in special classes in regular schools classified according to national categories All years of compulsory schooling**

STUDENTS IN NATIONAL CATEGORY 1. Name of category:

TYPE OF INSTITUTION	NUMBER OF INSTITUTIONS	NUMBER OF SPECIAL CLASSES	TEACHING STAFF			STUDENTS ENROLLED		
			Total full-time and part-time	Full-time	Full-time equivalents	Total males and females	Males	Females
	1	2	3 (4+5)	4	5	6 (7+8)	7	8
PRIMARY OR BASIC SCHOOL EDUCATION								
a1 Total public and private institutions (a2+a3)								
a2 Public institutions								
a3 All private institutions (a4+a5)								
a4 Government dependent private institutions								
a5 Independent private institutions								
SECONDARY EDUCATION								
a6 Total public and private institutions (a7+a8))								
a7 Public institutions								
a8 All private institutions (a9+a10)								
a9 Government dependent private institutions								
a10 Independent private institutions								
ALL YEARS OF COMPULSORY SCHOOLING								
a11 Total public and private institutions (a12+a13)								
a12 Public institutions								
a13 All private institutions (a14+a15)								
a14 Government dependent private institutions								
a15 Independent private institutions								

STUDENTS IN NATIONAL CATEGORY 2. Name of category:

Continuing up to category 20.

Table 3 (continued). **Students in special classes in regular schools**

STUDENTS IN ALL NATIONAL CATEGORIES CONSIDERED TO FALL WITHIN "RESOURCES" DEFINITION COMBINED

NOTE: the categories to be added to form entries in this part of the table are given by your responses to Q3 and Q4

TYPE OF INSTITUTION	NUMBER OF INSTITUTIONS	NUMBER OF SPECIAL CLASSES	TEACHING STAFF			STUDENTS ENROLLED		
			Total full-time and part-time	Full-time	Full-time equivalents	Total males and females	Males	Females
	161	162	163 (164+165)	164	165	166 (167+168)	167	168

PRIMARY OR BASIC SCHOOL EDUCATION

a1	Total public and private institutions	(a2+a3)
a2	Public institutions	
a3	All private institutions	(a4+a5)
a4	Government dependent private institutions	
a5	Independent private institutions	

SECONDARY EDUCATION

a6	Total public and private institutions	(a7+a8))
a7	Public institutions	
a8	All private institutions	(a9+a10)
a9	Government dependent private institutions	
a10	Independent private institutions	

ALL YEARS OF COMPULSORY SCHOOLING

a11	Total public and private institutions	(a12+a13)
a12	Public institutions	
a13	All private institutions	(a14+a15)
a14	Government dependent private institutions	
a15	Independent private institutions	

Table 3 (*continued*). **Students in special classes in regular schools**

STUDENTS IN ALL NATIONAL CATEGORIES OF SPECIAL EDUCATIONAL NEED COMBINED

Note: the categories to be added to form entries in this part of the table are given by your response to Q3

TYPE OF INSTITUTION	NUMBER OF INSTITUTIONS	NUMBER OF SPECIAL CLASSES	TEACHING STAFF			STUDENTS ENROLLED		
			Total full-time and part-time (172+173)	Full-time	Full-time equivalents	Total males and females (175+176)	Males	Females
	169	170	171	172	173	174	175	176
PRIMARY OR BASIC SCHOOL EDUCATION								
a1 Total public and private institutions (a2+a3)								
a2 Public institutions								
a3 All private institutions (a4+a5)								
a4 Government dependent private institutions								
a5 Independent private institutions								
SECONDARY EDUCATION								
a6 Total public and private institutions (a7+a8))								
a7 Public institutions								
a8 All private institutions (a9+a10)								
a9 Government dependent private institutions								
a10 Independent private institutions								
ALL YEARS OF COMPULSORY SCHOOLING								
a11 Total public and private institutions (a12+a13)								
a12 Public institutions								
a13 All private institutions (a14+a15)								
a14 Government dependent private institutions								
a15 Independent private institutions								

Table 4. **Information on programmes for students in regular classes in regular schools classified according to national categories**
All years of compulsory schooling

STUDENTS IN NATIONAL CATEGORY 1. Name of category:

TYPE OF INSTITUTION	NUMBER OF CLASSES INVOLVED	STUDENTS FALLING WITHIN NATIONAL CATEGORY		
		Total males and females (3+4)	Males	Females
	1	2	3	4

PRIMARY OR BASIC SCHOOL EDUCATION

a1	Total public and private institutions (a2+a3)				
a2	Public institutions				
a3	All private institutions (a4+a5)				
a4	Government dependent private institutions				
a5	Independent private institutions				

SECONDARY EDUCATION

a6	Total public and private institutions (a7+a8)				
a7	Public institutions				
a8	All private institutions (a9+a10)				
a9	Government dependent private institutions				
a10	Independent private institutions				

ALL YEARS OF COMPULSORY SCHOOLING

a11	Total public and private institutions (a12+a13)				
a12	Public institutions				
a13	All private institutions (a14+a15)				
a14	Government dependent private institutions				
a15	Independent private institutions				

STUDENTS IN NATIONAL CATEGORY 2. Name of category:

Continuing up to category 20.

Table 4 (*continued*). **Students in regular classes in regular schools**

STUDENTS IN ALL NATIONAL CATEGORIES CONSIDERED TO FALL WITHIN "RESOURCES" DEFINITION COMBINED

Note: the categories to be added to form entries in this part of the table are given by your responses to Q3 and Q4

TYPE OF INSTITUTION		NUMBER OF CLASSES INVOLVED	PROPORTION OF CLASSES INVOLVED	STUDENTS FALLING WITHIN NATIONAL CATEGORY		
				Total males and females	Males	Females
				(84+85)		
		81	82	83	84	85
PRIMARY OR BASIC SCHOOL EDUCATION						
a1	Total public and private institutions	(a2~a3)				
a2	Public institutions					
a3	All private institutions	(a4+a5)				
a4	Government dependent private institutions					
a5	Independent private institutions					
SECONDARY EDUCATION						
a6	Total public and private institutions	(a7+a8))				
a7	Public institutions					
a8	All private institutions	(a9+a10)				
a9	Government dependent private institutions					
a10	Independent private institutions					
ALL YEARS OF COMPULSORY SCHOOLING						
a11	Total public and private institutions	(a12+a13)				
a12	Public institutions					
a13	All private institutions	(a14+a15)				
a14	Government dependent private institutions					
a15	Independent private institutions					

Table 4 (continued). **Students in regular classes in regular schools**

STUDENTS IN ALL NATIONAL CATEGORIES OF SPECIAL EDUCATIONAL NEED COMBINED

Note: the categories to be added to form entries in this part of the table are given by your responses to Q3 andQ4

TYPE OF INSTITUTION		NUMBER OF CLASSES INVOLVED	PROPORTION OF CLASSES INVOLVED	STUDENTS FALLING WITHIN NATIONAL CATEGORY		
				Total males and females	Males	Females
				(84+85)		
		86	87	88	89	90

PRIMARY OR BASIC SCHOOL EDUCATION

a1	Total public and private institutions	(a2+a3)					
a2	Public institutions						
a3	All private institutions	(a4+a5)					
a4	Government dependent private institutions						
a5	Independent private institutions						

SECONDARY EDUCATION

a6	Total public and private institutions	(a7+a8)					
a7	Public institutions						
a8	All private institutions	(a9+a1C)					
a9	Government dependent private institutions						
a10	Independent private institutions						

ALL YEARS OF COMPULSORY SCHOOLING

a11	Total public and private institutions	(a12+a13)					
a12	Public institutions						
a13	All private institutions	(a14+a15					
a14	Government dependent private institutions						
a15	Independent private institutions						

131

Table 5. **Information on programmes in national categories by ISCED level for all years of compulsory schooling**

PROGRAMMES IN SPECIAL SCHOOLS

		TOTAL ENROLLED IN PROGRAMMES – PRE-PRIMARY LEVEL OF EDUCATION (ISCED LEVEL 0)	TOTAL ENROLLED IN PROGRAMMES – PRIMARY LEVEL OF EDUCATION (ISCED LEVEL 1)	TOTAL ENROLLED IN PROGRAMMES – LOWER SECONDARY LEVEL OF EDUCATION (ISCED LEVEL 2)	TOTAL ENROLLED IN PROGRAMMES – UPPER SECONDARY LEVEL OF EDUCATION (ISCED LEVEL 3)	TOTAL ENROLLED IN PROGRAMMES – PRE-PRIMARY, PRIMARY and SECONDARY LEVELS OF EDUCATION (ISCED LEVELS 0, 1, 2 and 3) (1+2+3+4)
	TOTAL PUBLIC and PRIVATE INSTITUTIONS	1	2	3	4	5
	National category					
a1	NC1:					
a2	NC2:					
a3	NC3:					
a4	NC4:					
a5	NC5:					
a6	NC6:					
a7	NC7:					
a8	NC8:					
a9	NC9:					
a10	NC10:					
a21	Total all national categories considered to fall within resources definition (the categories to be added to form entries in this part of the table are given by your responses to Q3 and Q4)					
a22	Total all national categories for special educational needs (the categories to be added to form entries in this part of the table are given by your response to Q3)					

Table 5 (*continued*). **Information on programmes in national categories by ISCED level for all years of compulsory schooling**

PROGRAMMES IN SPECIAL CLASSES IN REGULAR SCHOOLS

TOTAL PUBLIC and PRIVATE INSTITUTIONS

National category		TOTAL ENROLLED IN PROGRAMMES – PRE-PRIMARY LEVEL OF EDUCATION (ISCED LEVEL 0) 6	TOTAL ENROLLED IN PROGRAMMES – PRIMARY LEVEL OF EDUCATION (ISCED LEVEL 1) 7	TOTAL ENROLLED IN PROGRAMMES – LOWER SECONDARY LEVEL OF EDUCATION (ISCED LEVEL 2) 8	TOTAL ENROLLED IN PROGRAMMES – UPPER SECONDARY LEVEL OF EDUCATION (ISCED LEVEL 3) 9	TOTAL ENROLLED IN PROGRAMMES – PRE-PRIMARY, PRIMARY and SECONDARY LEVELS OF EDUCATION (ISCED LEVELS 0, 1, 2 and 3) 10 (6+7+8+9)
a1	NC1:					
a2	NC2:					
a3	NC3:					
a4	NC4:					
a5	NC5:					
a6	NC6:					
a7	NC7:					
a8	NC8:					
a9	NC9:					
a10	NC10:					
a21	Total all national categories considered to fall within resources definition (the categories to be added to form entries in this part of the table are given by your responses to Q3 and Q4)					
a22	Total all national categories for special educational needs (the categories to be added to form entries in this part of the table are given by your response to Q3)					

Table 5 (*continued*). **Information on programmes in national categories by ISCED level for all years of compulsory schooling**

PROGRAMMES IN SPECIAL CLASSES IN REGULAR SCHOOLS

National category	TOTAL ENROLLED IN PROGRAMMES – PRE-PRIMARY LEVEL OF EDUCATION (ISCED LEVEL 0) 11	TOTAL ENROLLED IN PROGRAMMES – PRIMARY LEVEL OF EDUCATION (ISCED LEVEL 1) 12	TOTAL ENROLLED IN PROGRAMMES – LOWER SECONDARY LEVEL OF EDUCATION (ISCED LEVEL 2) 13	TOTAL ENROLLED IN PROGRAMMES – UPPER SECONDARY LEVEL OF EDUCATION (ISCED LEVEL 3) 14	TOTAL ENROLLED IN PROGRAMMES – PRE-PRIMARY, PRIMARY and SECONDARY LEVELS OF EDUCATION (ISCED LEVELS 0, 1, 2 and 3) 15 (11+12+13+14)
TOTAL PUBLIC and PRIVATE INSTITUTIONS					
a1 NC1:					
a2 NC2:					
a3 NC3:					
a4 NC4:					
a5 NC5:					
a6 NC6:					
a7 NC7:					
a8 NC8:					
a9 NC9:					
a10 NC10:					
a21 Total all national categories considered to fall within resources definition	(the categories to be added to form entries in this part of the table are given by your responses to Q3 and Q4)				
a22 Total all national categories for special educational needs	(the categories to be added to form entries in this part of the table are given by your response to Q3)				

Table 5 (*continued*). **Information on programmes in national categories by ISCED level for all years of compulsory schooling**

PROGRAMMES IN REGULAR CLASSES IN REGULAR SCHOOLS

TOTAL PUBLIC and PRIVATE INSTITUTIONS

	National category	TOTAL ENROLLED IN PROGRAMMES – PRE-PRIMARY LEVEL OF EDUCATION (ISCED LEVEL 0) 16 (1+6+11)	TOTAL ENROLLED IN PROGRAMMES – PRIMARY LEVEL OF EDUCATION (ISCED LEVEL 1) 17 (2+7+12)	TOTAL ENROLLED IN PROGRAMMES – LOWER SECONDARY LEVEL OF EDUCATION (ISCED LEVEL 2) 18 (3+8+13)	TOTAL ENROLLED IN PROGRAMMES – UPPER SECONDARY LEVEL OF EDUCATION (ISCED LEVEL 3) 19 (4+9+14)	TOTAL ENROLLED IN PROGRAMMES – PRE-PRIMARY, PRIMARY and SECONDARY LEVELS OF EDUCATION (ISCED LEVELS 0, 1, 2 and 3) 20 (16+17+18+19)
a1	NC1:					
a2	NC2:					
a3	NC3:					
a4	NC4:					
a5	NC5:					
a6	NC6:					
a7	NC7:					
a8	NC8:					
a9	NC9:					
a10	NC10:					
a21	Total all national categories considered to fall within resources definition	(the categories to be added to form entries in this part of the table are given by your responses to Q3 and Q4)				
a22	Total all national categories for special educational needs	(the categories to be added to form entries in this part of the table are given by your response to Q3)				

Table 6. **Information on students enrolled in programmes by age**

ALL NATIONAL CATEGORIES FALLING WITHIN "RESOURCES" DEFINITION

Reference date for age (day/month)   /

NOTE: the categories to be added to form entries in this part of the table are given by your responses to Q3 and Q4

TOTAL PUBLIC and PRIVATE INSTITUTIONS	AGE GROUPS	TOTAL ENROLLED IN PROGRAMMES IN SPECIAL SCHOOLS			TOTAL ENROLLED IN PROGRAMMES IN SPECIAL CLASSES IN REGULAR SCHOOLS			TOTAL ENROLLED IN PROGRAMMES IN REGULAR CLASSES IN REGULAR SCHOOLS			TOTAL ENROLLED IN PROGRAMMES IN ALL SETTINGS		
		Total males and females	Males	Females	Total males and females	Males	Females	Total males and females	Males	Females	Total males and females	Males	Females
		1	2	3	4	5	6	7	8	9	10	11	12
		(2+3)			(5+6)			(8+9)			(11+12)	(2+5+8)	(3+6+9)
a1	Total all age groups (a2 to a14)+a20												
a2	Under 3years												
a3	3 years												
a4	4 years												
a5	5 years												
a6	6 years												
a7	7 years												
a8	8 years												
a9	9 years												
a10	10 years												
a11	11 years												
a12	12 years												
a13	13 years												
a14	14 years												
a15	15 years												
a16	16 years												
a17	17 years												
a18	18 years												
a19	19 years												
a20	Subtotal 15-19 years (a15 to a19)												
a21	Subtotal – years of compulsory schooling												

Table 6 (*continued*). **Information on students enrolled in programmes by age**

ALL NATIONAL CATEGORIES OF SPECIAL EDUCATIONAL NEEDS

Reference date for age (day/month)

NOTE: the categories to be added to form entries in this part of the table are given by your responses to Q3 and Q4

TOTAL PUBLIC and PRIVATE INSTITUTIONS	AGE GROUPS	TOTAL ENROLLED IN PROGRAMMES IN SPECIAL SCHOOLS			TOTAL ENROLLED IN PROGRAMMES IN SPECIAL CLASSES IN REGULAR SCHOOLS			TOTAL ENROLLED IN PROGRAMMES IN REGULAR CLASSES IN REGULAR SCHOOLS			TOTAL ENROLLED IN PROGRAMMES IN ALL SETTINGS		
		Total males and females	Males	Females	Total males and females	Males	Females	Total males and females	Males	Females	Total males and females	Males	Females
		13	14	15	16	17	18	19	20	21	22	23	24
		(14+15)			(17+18)			(20+21)			(23+24)	(14+17+0)	(15+18+21)
a1	Total all age groups (a2 to a14)+a20												
a2	Under 3 years												
a3	3 years												
a4	4 years												
a5	5 years												
a6	6 years												
a7	7 years												
a8	8 years												
a9	9 years												
a10	10 years												
a11	11 years												
a12	12 years												
a13	13 years												
a14	14 years												
a15	15 years												
a16	16 years												
a17	17 years												
a18	18 years												
a19	19 years												
a20	Subtotal 15-19 years (a15 to a19)												
a21	Subtotal – years of compulsory schooling												

Table 7. **Relative resourcing for special educational needs**

ALL NATIONAL CATEGORIES CONSIDERED TO FALL WITHIN THE RESOURCES DEFINITION

NOTE: the categories to be added to form entries in this table are given by your responses to Q3 and Q4

	PERSONNEL			Financial
	Teachers	Professional	Indirect support	
	1	2	3	4

PRIMARY OR BASIC SCHOOL EDUCATION

a1	Programmes in special schools			
a2	Special classes in regular schools			
a3	Regular classes in regular schools			

SECONDARY EDUCATION

a4	Programmes in special schools			
a5	Special classes in regular schools			
a6	Regular classes in regular schools			

Table 7 (*continued*). **Relative resourcing for special educational needs for cross-national categories A, B, and C (falling within the resources definition)**

ALL YEARS OF COMPULSORY SCHOOLING

	PERSONNEL			
	Teachers	Professional	Indirect support	Financial
	1	2	3	4

CROSS-NATIONAL CATEGORY A

a7	Programmes in special schools			
a8	Special classes in regular schools			
a9	Regular classes in regular schools			

CROSS-NATIONAL CATEGORY B

a10	Programmes in special schools			
a11	Special classes in regular schools			
a12	Regular classes in regular schools			

CROSS-NATIONAL CATEGORY C

a13	Programmes in special schools			
a14	Special classes in regular schools			
a15	Regular classes in regular schools			

CROSS-NATIONAL CATEGORIES COMBINED

a16	Programmes in special schools			
a17	Special classes in regular schools			
a18	Regular classes in regular schools			

Annex 4

NOTES ON DATA TABLES

Initial note for systems where categories of special educational needs are not used in collecting data

It will be apparent that the data tables assume the existence of data about national categories relevant to programmes for students with special educational needs. If you do not collect this type of data it is clearly difficult for you to respond. It may, however, be feasible to use the tables creatively so that worthwhile information can be presented in this format. You are invited to make use of **estimation**, or of substitution of the term "category" for others used in your system, and of extensive **annotation** (see below) (*sample annotation sheets are attached as Annex 5*).

General notes

The tables are at the same time much less complex and substantially more difficult to complete than they may appear at first sight. They are less complex because the large number of possible national categories of special educational needs which are provided will generate many "not applicable" responses in most countries. The tables go to a level of detail which will be captured in some systems of national data collection but not in others. They may be difficult because, while every effort has been made to call for data in ways that mirror national approaches, there will inevitably be problems of interpretation because of the wide diversity of national systems and terminologies.

The following general principles apply:

- Whenever feasible enter data into all cells of a table which apply to your system;

- Some cells call for summaries of data which is provided in other cells (these cells are shaded in the tables). It may be that you can provide the summary data, even if there is not information for individual cells. For example, if gender information is not collected (*i.e.* separate data for males and females) the "total males and females" cells can still be used.

> Where national statistics are not available for particular cells, parts of tables, or whole tables, you are invited to contribute any findings from sample studies, projects, etc., which appear to be of relevance.

Variation in numbers of national categories of special educational needs

There is substantial variation from country to country in the number of categories of special educational needs which are used in the collection of data. The questionnaire allowed for systems which have up to twenty such categories (fifteen possible national categories of special educational needs [Q3], and five possible categories falling within the resources definition [Q4]). Allowing for this number of national categories in the data tables would produce very cumbersome tables and as most countries have ten or fewer national categories the data tables have been standardised to allow for up to ten categories To cope with systems that have more than ten national categories, extension tables have been provided allowing for a total of twenty categories. *The extension tables should be ignored if ten or fewer national categories are used.*

Within country variation

It is appreciated that in some countries there will be substantial differences in various aspects of special educational needs provision in different parts of the country (*e.g.* in Switzerland or the United States of America where the second

141

tier of government has substantial autonomy in matters relating to education). The data collection tables call for natio-nal averages, but annotations should be made drawing attention to any such within country variation.

If more detailed data are available (*e.g.* giving statistics for individual regions, states, etc.) you are invited to include this *in addition to* the national data. Copies of the various data collection tables can be made and used for this purpose with appropriate changes to the table title.

Technical notes for the completion of the tables

These notes are based on instructions in the UOE Data Collection Exercise but are considerably simplified. Please always keep in mind the following essentials:

Do **not** leave cells of the tables blank. Each cell in a table must be filled out either with a valid data value or with one of the missing codes described below. **IF, HOWEVER, YOU HAVE FEWER THAN TEN NATIONAL CATEGORIES (as indi-cated in answers to Q3 and Q4) IT IS ACCEPTABLE IN TABLES 2, 3 and 4 TO COMPLETE AND RETURN ONLY THOSE SHEETS APPROPRIATE TO THE NUMBER OF YOUR CATEGORIES.**

Do **not** enter any value other than numbers or the pre-defined missing codes (see below). Do not insert any strings (*e.g.* do not use "8" or '8' but only 8).

Do **not** use 0 (zero) as a code, use the missing codes "category not applicable" or "magnitude nil" instead (see below).

Verify the consistency of the data within and between the tables. You will find indications for such checks in the data collection tables. For example, for sub-totals it will usually be indicated through the column- and row-codes which data categories they comprise.

Unless stated otherwise, data in this study refer to **FULL-TIME STUDENTS ONLY**

Identification codes

All rows and columns in each table have been assigned a code so that each cell can be uniquely identified by the table identification and the corresponding row- and column-codes.

Shaded and non-shaded cells

Non-shaded (White) cells are base-cells which should be completed with either a valid data value or one of the missing codes.

Shaded cells are ones which are derived from base-cells.

Notes on the coding of missing data

The correct use of the missing codes is an *essential* condition to ensure the integrity of the data. The different rea-sons as to why there are no data in a particular instance need to be distinguished in the statistical analyses and the reports, and must therefore be distinguished in the data tables.

Each cell for which there is no valid data value must be assigned one of the following five missing codes:

a   Category not applicable because the category does not apply.

m   Data missing.

n   Magnitude is either nil or negligible.

x   Data included in another category/column of the table.

Category not applicable (a)

If a certain category or cell in the tables generically does not apply to the educational system(s) in your country then assign the code "**a**" to all cells referring to this category (or cross-classification of categories). This implies that data for these categories do not even hypothetically exist.

- For example if you have five national categories for special educational needs, then in Tables 2, 3 and 4 information asked for in relation to categories 6, 7, 8, 9 and 10 is "not applicable".

However, if a category applies but there are no data available or if the data for this category are included in another category then do **not** use this code.

- For example, if in a country there are no independent private schools, then for all variables the cells referring to independent private schools should be assigned the code "**a**".

If, on the other hand, independent private schools do exist but data are not available for these, then one of the other missing codes must be used.

- For example, if the data for independent private schools are included in the data referring to the total of all private schools then the sub-categories referring independent private schools should be coded to "included in another category" instead.

You should provide an annotation to categories which are not applicable to your education system.

Data missing (m)

Sometimes data are generally not available for certain classification categories and are not included in any other cells of the table (even though these data could, in principle, be collected). In such cases, you should assign the code "**m**" to all cells referring to the corresponding classification categories.

However, if the data for these classification categories are included in other categories of the tables or in the corresponding row- and column-totals, then do not use the code "**m**" but use an "**x**"-code instead.

Magnitude either nil (n) or negligible (n...)

If a data value is nil then assign the code "**n**" to the corresponding cell.

If a category is not applicable and therefore the data value would be zero for a cell, then do not use the code "**n**" but use the code "**a**" for "category not applicable" instead.

Do not use the value 0 (zero) to indicate that a value is nil.

In other cases, data may not be available but the magnitude may be known to be negligible with respect to the values in the other categories of this variable. Such instances should be assigned the code "**n<magnitude>**" (i.e. "**n**" followed by an indication of the estimated magnitude).

For example, if the value of a category is estimated to be smaller than 120, then the code would be "**nl20**".

This will be important when such data are used for international comparisons because, obviously, a value which is negligible in the United States may not be negligible in Luxembourg.

For example, some countries have very small numbers of independent private schools for which they collect no data but they may know that there are less than 120 teachers employed in such schools as compared to 325 000 teachers in

OECD 2000

government dependent private and public schools. In such case the code **nl20** would be assigned to the categories of educational personnel in independent private schools.

Data included in other categories (x)

Sometimes certain data are not available (even though the corresponding categories apply) but the data are included in other categories of the tables. Most frequently this occurs in situations where data are not available for certain sub-categories and can be provided for sub totals or totals only. The target category may thereby be in another row of the table, in another column of the table, or in another row *and* column.

If data are not available for certain sub-categories but the data for these sub-categories are included in the corresponding row- and column-totals of the data collection tables then enter the code "**x**" into all of the corresponding cells. Please supply a separate textual annotation which indicates in which category or categories the data are included.

If a category is not applicable, then do not use any of the "**x**" codes but use the code "**a**" instead.

Provisional or estimated data

In some situations, countries may not have precise data available for certain categories of certain variables but it may still be possible to provide an estimate or a provisional substitute for these data.

Examples of such situations are:

- a country may collect no data on a variable but can create an estimate based on assumed relationships to other variables;

- a country may not have data on the desired level of aggregation but may be able to provide aggregate figures on the basis of assumed relationships to other variables For example, data may not be available at the national level, but can be aggregated from state or provincial figures);

- data may be available only for certain sub-populations but estimates can be provided for the remainder for example, certain data may be available for public schools and government-dependent private schools but not for independent private schools); or

- data may not be available for the year of the data collection but it may be possible to provide a provisional estimate on the basis of data from previous years.

It is essential that data providers make every effort to correctly estimate the data in such instances. If data are missing for a particular classification category, this often means that the data for the whole variable cannot be used for that country or that crude assumptions about the missing data have to be made when analysing the data. It is clear that such assumptions, if made centrally without the supplementary information that may be available in the countries, are often problematic.

- for example, if there are independent private schools in a country but there are no data for these, and therefore the country includes in the data only the data for public schools and government dependent private schools, then the data for that country will be biased. It will be impossible to account for and adjust this data in the international analyses. If, on the other hand, the country can provide an estimate for the independent private schools then corresponding adjustments can be made in the international comparative analyses.

If data are provisional or estimated, or if there are discrepancies between the international data definitions and the national data definitions applied, then data providers should annotate these instances correspondingly.

Estimated figures should be preceded by an "e" in the cell, and an **annotation** made (see below).

For example

e 240	

Annotations

If you wish to make a comment about the entry made for a particular cell or cells this is known as an annotation. Such annotations should be presented on a separate "Annotation Sheets" (see Annex 5). Reference should be made to the table referred to and the specific cell(s) using the letter and number defining the row and column of the sheet.

For example:

		NUMBER OF INSTITUTIONS	TEACHING STAFF Total full-time and part-time
		1	2
	TYPE OF INSTITUTION		(3+4)
a1	Total public and private institutions	(a2+a3)	
a2	Public institutions	e240	

The "e 240" is in cell in row "a2" and column "1" and hence should be referred to on the annotation sheet as "Table 2 a2/1". For several cells use "a2-a6/1" or "a5/6-10", etc.

Annotations should always be used when it has been necessary to estimate data, giving the basis for the estimation. However, they can be used at any time to comment on the data given (or not given).

For example, annotations allow data providers:

- to document national deviations from the international definitions of underlying variables and classification categories;

- to provide information on the kind of estimation undertaken, and the estimation procedure used in those cases where provisional or estimated data were reported (in particular, an indication of the methods of calculation undertaken if the values are aggregates or derived from other variables);

- to provide an evaluation of the accuracy of the estimates.

Notes on individual tables

Table 1. Information on years of compulsory schooling

COMPULSORY SCHOOLING refers to the period of years for which attendance at a school is required by law or regulation. A school is an institution whose prime function is education. In the special educational needs field this may include a variety of institutions, which may be referred to as centres, units, etc., as well as schools.

This table calls for data on the years of compulsory schooling for students following special educational needs programmes in both segregated and integrated settings, and corresponding data on regular programmes. While these years of schooling may be the same for students in all settings this is not the case in all countries. If schooling is not compul-

145

sory in your system then you should provide an annotation indicating this and the basis for the selection of starting and ending ages, which should be the closest equivalent to compulsory schooling relevant to your system.

REFERENCE DATE/PERIOD FOR DATA COLLECTION (MONTH and YEAR) is the date/period in which institutions, students, personnel, etc., were counted, or in which other statistics were collected. This should be for your **1996 data collection** which it is assumed will in most countries now be fully analysed. If the data are only available for an earlier year, please enter those data – if possible also giving an **estimate** for the 1996 data. If most of the data refers to 1996 but some data are only available for an earlier year, use 1996 data where possible and indicate in the appropriate table where earlier data have been used, again giving an **estimate** for 1996 data where possible.

THEORETICAL STARTING AGE (OF PRIMARY OR BASIC SCHOOL EDUCATION) is the age as established by law and regulation for the entry to the first compulsory or required cycle of school education. It is the age at the beginning of the first school year of the cycle. Pre-school education is, by definition, excluded.

THEORETICAL ENDING AGE OF PRIMARY OR BASIC SCHOOL EDUCATION is the age as established by law and regulation for the ending of the first compulsory or required cycle of school education. It is the age at the beginning of the last school year of the cycle.

THEORETICAL ENDING AGE OF GENERALLY REQUIRED SCHOOL EDUCATION is the age as established by law and regulation for the ending of the final compulsory or required cycle of school education. It is the age at the beginning of the last school year of the cycle. The theoretical ending age relates to the theoretical duration assuming full-time attendance in the education system and assuming that no year is repeated. Later stages or cycles of education, where there is an expectation that some students may not continue in education, should be excluded.

Note that the theoretical ages may differ significantly from the typical ages. If there are regional differences in the theoretical ages or if these differ by other criteria, then the weighted averages should be given for the theoretical ages.

YEARS OF COMPULSORY SCHOOLING are the years from **theoretical starting age** of school education, to **theoretical ending age** of generally required school education. Typically, this will cover primary education and some, or all, of secondary education, but ages and types of organisation will differ from country to country, and possibly, from programme to programme.

REGULAR EDUCATION PROGRAMMES are programmes in regular classes in regular, mainstream, schools.

SPECIAL EDUCATIONAL NEEDS PROGRAMMES IN SPECIAL SCHOOLS are programmes for students with special educational needs enrolled in special schools (*i.e.* in segregated settings).

SPECIAL EDUCATIONAL NEEDS PROGRAMMES IN SPECIAL CLASSES IN REGULAR SCHOOLS are programmes for students with special educational needs for which provision is made in special classes or units attached to regular, mainstream, schools. It is a special class or unit only if it is administratively within the regular school. If the unit is administered separately it is classified as a special school.

SPECIAL EDUCATIONAL NEEDS PROGRAMMES IN REGULAR CLASSES IN REGULAR SCHOOLS are programmes for students with special educational needs for which provision is made in regular classes in regular, mainstream, schools.

Table 2. Information on programmes for students in special schools classified according to national categories

This table calls for data on the numbers of students and teachers in institutions classified as special schools for different national categories of special educational need.

ALL YEARS OF COMPULSORY SCHOOLING are from "Theoretical starting age of primary or basic school education" to "Theoretical ending age of generally required school education" as specified in Table 1 for Special Educational Needs Programmes in Special Schools. It is restricted to these years as pilot work established the relative inadequacy of data on special educational needs at pre-primary and post-compulsory stages.

PRIMARY OR BASIC SCHOOL EDUCATION is from "Theoretical starting age of primary or basic school education" to "Theoretical ending age of primary or basic school education" as specified in Table 1 for Special Educational Needs Programmes in Special Schools.

SECONDARY EDUCATION is from "Theoretical ending age of primary or basic school education" to "Theoretical ending age of generally required school education" as specified in Table 1 for Special Educational Needs Programmes in Special Schools.

IMPORTANT: You are asked to use the categories of special educational need for which data are collected in your national system (as given in answer to Q3 in Section 1) AND those given in answer to Q4 (*i.e.* national categories which you consider to fall within the "resources" definition even though they do not fall within your definition of special educational needs). All national categories of special educational need should be entered in the table (*i.e.* both those considered to fall within the "resources" definition of special educational needs and any which are not considered to do so).

For example, IF you have indicated:

1) in Q3 that you have *five* national categories of special educational needs, and consider that the first four fall within the "resources" definition but the fifth one does not, AND

2) in Q4 that there is *one* further national category which you consider to fall within the "resources" definition, but not within your definition of special educational needs, THEN

3) All *six* national categories should be entered in Table 2

If there are fewer than ten national categories you need only complete and return those sheets appropriate to the number of national categories (see 3.5 above). If there are more than ten national categories please use the appropriate number of the extension sheets provided.

Note: **Multiple categorisation.** It is appreciated that some categorisation systems allow for the possibility of multiple categorisation (*e.g.* by considering a student to fall within two or more categories, and counting such students on a whole or fractional basis for separate categories; or by creating separate multiple categories for relatively frequent combinations). Any form of multiple categorisation other than that obvious in the name and description (*e.g.* deaf-blind) should be annotated and explained.

PUBLIC INSTITUTIONS refers to educational institutions which are controlled and managed directly by a public education authority or agency, or by a governing body (Council, Committee, etc.), most of whose members are either appointed by a public authority or elected by public franchise.

PRIVATE INSTITUTIONS refers to educational institutions which are controlled and managed by a non-governmental organisation (*e.g.* a Church, a Trade Union or a business enterprise), or if its Governing Board consists mostly of persons not selected by a public agency.

Various types of private institution make a substantial contribution to provision for special educational needs in many countries. Where such contributions exist it will be appreciated if every effort is made to incorporate relevant data (on an estimated basis if necessary). If such data are not accessible an annotation should be made.

GOVERNMENT DEPENDENT PRIVATE INSTITUTIONS refers to the degree of a private institution's dependence on funding from private sources. It is considered government dependent if it receives more than 50% of its core funding from government agencies. Core funding refers to funds that support the basic educational services of the institution. It does not include fees and subsidies received for ancillary services, such as lodging or meals. Additionally, institutions should be considered as government dependent if their teaching personnel are paid by a government agency – either directly or through government.

INDEPENDENT PRIVATE INSTITUTIONS refers to private institutions which do not receive more than 50% of their core funding from government agencies, nor are their teaching personnel are paid by a government agency – either directly or through government.

> Here (and in later tables) responses should not be limited to institutions supported by ministries or departments of education if other ministries (*e.g.* social services, employment or labour) have an educational involvement in special educational needs. Where it is known that such involvement exists it will be appreciated if every effort is made to incorporate relevant data (on an estimated basis if necessary). If such data are not accessible an annotation should be made.

NUMBER OF INSTITUTIONS refers to the number of special schools which enrol students with that particular category of special educational need. A school catering exclusively for that category counts in full. A school catering for more than one category counts proportionately:

- For example, a school with 50% students in category 1; 30% in category 3, and 20% in category 4 should contribute 0.5 to category 1, 0.3 to category 3, and 0.2 to category 4.

TEACHING STAFF refers to persons whose professional activity involves the transmission of knowledge, attitudes and skills as stipulated to students in a specified educational programme. It does not depend on the qualification held by the teacher. The following should be excluded: those without active teaching duties; those who only work occasionally, or in a voluntary capacity; and those providing services other than formal instruction to students. Senior staff without teaching responsibilities are not to be counted. Persons with teaching and administrative duties should be pro-rated where possible; if this is not possible they should be classified as teachers if the majority of their working time is spent teaching. Teaching staff in a school catering for more than one category of special educational need should be pro rated.

FULL-TIME refers to a head count of teaching staff who are teaching on a full-time basis in relation to a specific category of special educational need.

FULL-TIME EQUIVALENTS refers exclusively to teaching staff who are not teaching on a full-time basis. It includes both those who have responsibilities in addition to teaching, those employed to teach on a part-time basis, and those who teach students from more than one category of special educational need. Contributions should be pro rated.

For example, A principal whose teaches 20% of her time, three senior teachers teaching 40% of their time and three part-time teachers on 50% contracts would total 2.9 full-time equivalents (0.2+ [3 x 0.4] + [3 x 0.5])

STUDENTS ENROLLED refers to the count of students enrolled during the reference period. Each student enrolled in the educational programme should be counted once and only once. It is assumed that all students are enrolled on a full-time basis. Please annotate appropriately if this is not the case. Students who spend a proportion of their time in a regular school or other setting should still be counted on a full basis unless there is a formal arrangement where the student is enrolled at a second institution when pro rating should be used.

> In the two summary sections on the final sheet of the table, the first refers to totals for students in all national categories considered to fall within the "resources" definition (*i.e.* those for which a "yes" answer was given in the right hand column for Q3 AND those given in answer to Q4).The final section refers to totals for students in all national categories of special educational needs as entered for Q3 (*i.e.* whether or not they are considered to fall within the "resources" definition).

Table 3. Information on programmes for students in special classes in regular schools classified according to national categories

This table calls for the same information as Table 2, but in relation to special classes in regular schools. The same general rubrics apply. **IN PARTICULAR, THE SAME NATIONAL CATEGORIES AS IN TABLE 2 SHOULD BE INCLUDED.**

ALL YEARS OF COMPULSORY SCHOOLING are from "Theoretical starting age of primary or basic school education" to "Theoretical ending age of generally required school education" as specified in Table 1 for Special Educational Needs Programmes in Special Classes in Regular Schools.

PRIMARY OR BASIC SCHOOL EDUCATION is from "Theoretical starting age of primary or basic school education" to "Theoretical ending age of primary or basic school education" as specified in Table 1 for Special Educational Needs Programmes in Special Classes in Regular Schools.

SECONDARY EDUCATION is from "Theoretical ending age of primary or basic school education" to "Theoretical ending age of generally required school education" as specified in Table 1 for Special Educational Needs Programmes in Special Classes in Regular Schools.

SPECIAL CLASSES refers to programmes for students with special educational needs which are organised on the basis of a special class, or special unit, in a regular or mainstream school. To qualify as a special class, students should be regarded as enrolled in the regular school and the special class fall within the administration of the regular school. If these conditions do not apply the class is effectively a segregated unit and should be entered in Table 2 above as a special school. Students enrolled in special classes who spend part of their time in regular classes or in other settings should still be counted on a full basis but this should be annotated.

NUMBER OF SPECIAL CLASSES refers to the total number of special classes which enrol students with a particular category of special educational need. A class catering exclusively for that category counts in full. A class catering for more than one category counts proportionately:

- For example, a class with 80% students in category 1; and 20% in category 4 should contribute 0.8 to category 1 and 0.2 to category 4.

NUMBER OF INSTITUTIONS in this context refers to the number of regular schools which have one or more special classes for students with a particular category of special educational need. In the parts of the tables covering individual categories, the number of institutions recorded should be the number of regular schools which have at least one special class which caters for that specific category of special educational need (even if it also caters for another category or categories of special educational need).

> In the two summary sections on the final sheet of the table, the first refers to totals for students in all national categories considered to fall within the "resources" definition (*i.e.* those for which a "yes" answer was given in the right hand column for Q3 AND those given in answer to Q4). Here the number of institutions recorded should be the total number of schools with special classes in any of the relevant categories. The final section refers to totals for students in all national categories of special educational needs as entered for Q3 (*i.e.* whether or not they are considered to fall within the "resources" definition). Again the number of institutions recorded should be the total number of schools with special classes in any of the national categories. To the extent that schools have more than one special class, and/or that special classes cater for more than one special educational need, the total numbers of schools will be less than the sum of the numbers of schools in the different separate categories.

Table 4. Information on programmes for students in regular classes in regular schools classified according to national categories

This table calls for much of the same information as in Tables 2 and 3, but in relation to regular classes in regular schools. The same general rubrics apply. **IN PARTICULAR, THE SAME NATIONAL CATEGORIES AS IN TABLES 2 and 3 SHOULD BE INCLUDED.**

ALL YEARS OF COMPULSORY SCHOOLING are from "Theoretical starting age of primary or basic school education" to "Theoretical ending age of generally required school education" as specified in Table 1 for Special Educational Needs Programmes in Regular Classes in Regular Schools.

PRIMARY OR BASIC SCHOOL EDUCATION is from "Theoretical starting age of primary or basic school education" to "Theoretical ending age of primary or basic school education" as specified in Table 1 for Special Educational Needs Programmes in Regular Classes in Regular Schools.

SECONDARY EDUCATION is from "Theoretical ending age of primary or basic school education" to "Theoretical ending age of generally required school education" as specified in Table 1 for Special Educational Needs Programmes in Regular Classes in Regular Schools.

PROGRAMMES FOR STUDENTS IN REGULAR CLASSES IN REGULAR SCHOOLS refers to the situation where it is accepted that a regular classroom includes one or more students falling within the national categories of special educational needs and/or the "resources" definition. The students may have been individually identified through a formal process or their presence inferred or assumed though some theoretical model or other basis of planning.

NUMBER OF CLASSES INVOLVED refers to the number of classes which include one or more students falling within the national categories of special educational needs and/or the "resources" definition of special educational needs.

STUDENTS FALLING WITHIN NATIONAL CATEGORY refers to the count of students enrolled during the reference period where individual identification makes this feasible. If students' presence has been inferred or assumed in planning please provide an **estimate,** preceding the entry with "e" to indicate its status and annotating to indicate the basis of the estimate.

In the two summary sections on the final sheet of the table, the first refers to totals for students in all national categories considered to fall within the "resources" definition (*i.e.* those for which a "yes" answer was given in the right hand column for Q3 AND those given in answer to Q4).The final section refers to totals for students in all national categories of special educational needs as entered for Q3 (*i.e.* whether or not they are considered to fall within the "resources" definition). These sections incorporate an additional column on the proportion of classes involved.

PROPORTION OF CLASSES INVOLVED refers to the proportion of classes which include one or more students falling within one or more of the combined categories (*i.e.* the number of classes involved expressed as a proportion of the total number of classes in schools of the given type *in the national system overall*).

Table 5. Information on programmes for students in national categories by ISCED *level in all settings and for all years of compulsory education.*

The table is similar in format to earlier ones and the same general conventions apply. It calls for information about the allocation of programmes for students in different national categories to level of education as indexed in ISCED. **YOU SHOULD AGAIN INCLUDE THE SAME NATIONAL CATEGORIES AS IN TABLES 2, 3 and 4.**

ISCED is the International Standard Classification of Education which was initially designed by UNESCO in the early 1970s to serve as an instrument suitable for assembling, compiling and presenting statistics of education both within countries and internationally. It is currently undergoing a process of updating and revision. ISCED is used in the general UOE Data Collection Exercise and it would be of considerable value if it were possible to link it to Special Educational Needs programmes.

ISCED LEVELS provide a standardised means of classifying educational programmes. For the purposes of this study the relevant levels appear to be:

LEVEL 0 – Pre-Primary Education

LEVEL 1 – Primary Education or First Stage of Basic Education

LEVEL 2 – Lower Secondary or Second Stage of Basic Education

LEVEL 3 – Upper Secondary Education

Annex 2 gives an explanation of the way in which these levels are to be interpreted. Detailed attention should be given to the defining characteristics of these levels when assigning programmes to levels.

NOTE that the data to be entered in the table covers ALL settings (*i.e.* special schools, special classes in regular schools, and regular classes in regular schools) and ALL YEARS OF COMPULSORY EDUCATION (*i.e.* as indicated in Table 1, and used in Tables 2, 3 and 4). Note in particular that age of the students involved does not in itself necessarily determine level (*e.g.* a programme for students falling within a particular national category of special educational need might be at Level 0 even though the students involved are above the starting age for school attendance). Do not include children below the starting age for school attendance who are involved in Level 0 programmes (however an annotation should be made if there is provision for such children). Do not include students on Level 3 programmes if they are above the age of generally required school attendance as indicated in Table 1.

If this rubric is followed the TOTAL ENROLLED IN PROGRAMMES FOR ISCED LEVELS 0, 1, 2 and 3 (right hand column of the table) for each national category, and for combined categories, should be the same total as the combined totals for that category from Tables 2, 3 and 4.

For example, in connection with national category 1 the entry for row "all" and column "5" in Table 2 (Table 2 a11/5) should be the same as that for row "a1" and column "5" in Table 5 (Table 5 a1/5). Similarly, for all national categories considered to fall within the resources definition combined, the entry for row "all" and column "145" in Table 2 (Table 2 a11/145) should be the same as that for row "a21" and column "5" in Table 5 (Table 5 a21/5).

Table 6. Information on students enrolled in programmes by age

This table asks for information on programmes for students with special educational needs by age in the same format as that of the current UOE data collection exercise. That exercise was limited to programmes for students with special educational needs in special schools, and the attempt is made here to extend this to cover programmes for students with special educational needs in other settings.

TOTAL ENROLLED IN PROGRAMMES IN SPECIAL SCHOOLS refers to the number of students of that age in this setting.

TOTAL ENROLLED IN PROGRAMMES IN SPECIAL CLASSES IN REGULAR SCHOOLS refers to the number of students of that age in this setting.

TOTAL ENROLLED IN PROGRAMMES IN REGULAR CLASSES IN REGULAR SCHOOLS refers to the number of students of that age in this setting.

TOTAL ENROLLED IN PROGRAMMES refers to the number of students of that age in all settings.

The first part of the table asks for totals covering national categories of special educational need which fall within the "resources" definition (*i.e.* to which the answer "yes" was given in response to Q3) together with any other categories considered to fall within the resources definition (*i.e.* those given in answer to Q4). The second part asks for totals covering all national categories of special educational needs (*i.e.* the total set of categories given in answer to Q3 including any considered to fall outside the resources definition as well as those falling within it).

If this task is not feasible and some other basis has to be used, annotations should be given indicating the basis adopted.

REFERENCE DATE FOR AGE (DAY/MONTH) refers to the date to which student ages are referred (normally taken as December 31st).

AGE is the difference between the year of observation and the year of the person's birth if the reference date is taken as December 31st. If available data refer to age at some other date then enrolment data should be distributed across ages on the basis of estimation. Please annotate if this is done.

To maintain comparability with the corresponding table in the UOE data collection

a) "under 3 years" and other early years categories have been included in this table. For students in these younger age groups to be included the programmes must have a substantial educational component – see Annex 2 giving ISCED definitions. If national statistics are linked to a broader definition of pre-primary education please annotate.

b) Similarly the table asks for data on pupils up to and including 19 years of age which is in most countries above the ending age of generally required school education.

To maintain comparability with other tables this table asks for data on **FULL-TIME STUDENTS ONLY.** The corresponding table in the UOE data collection asks for both full and part time numbers. If data are available on part time numbers please annotate

> *Note*: The last row in the table asks for sub-totals corresponding to Years of Compulsory Schooling which will be as indicated in Table 1 (which may vary for special school, special class and regular class settings.
>
> As a cross-check, these sub-totals for different settings, and the total for all settings, should be the same as the corresponding totals in Table 5.
>
> For example, in connection with programmes in special schools, the entry for row a21 and column 5 in Table 5 (Table 5 a21/5) should be the same as that for row a21 and column 1 in Table 6 (Table 6 a21/1). Similarly, for all settings combined, the entry for row a21 and column 20 in Table 5 (Table 5 a21/20) should be the same as that for row a21 and column 10 in Table 6 (Table 6 a21/20).

Table 7. Information on relative resourcing for special educational needs

This table seeks information on the amount of additional resources made available to students following programmes for students with special educational needs. The resources to be considered are those which are in support of their education. While this should be interpreted widely it excludes resources where this educational link can not be explicitly demonstrated. It is accepted that full quantification of all such resources is an extremely complex and difficult task. However, pilot work has established the feasibility of making an assessment of the relative resourcing of programmes for students with special educational needs and regular education programmes.

ALL NATIONAL CATEGORIES CONSIDERED TO FALL WITHIN THE RESOURCES DEFINITION – as in previous tables this refers to the national categories of special educational needs considered to fall within the resources definition (as indicated in response to Q3) **AND** any other categories considered to fall within the resources definition (Q4).

RELATIVE RESOURCING refers to the resourcing of programmes for this category of special educational need in this setting relative to programmes of regular education in a typical non-residential school setting. This should be expressed as a ratio.

- For example, if resourcing of programmes of regular education is taken as a base of 100, and resourcing of programmes for students with special educational needs is 50% greater than this (*i.e.* 150) then the ratio to be given is 1.5. These figures will typically be estimates and should be indicated as such and annotated.

PRIMARY OR BASIC SCHOOL EDUCATION is from "Theoretical starting age of primary or basic school education" to "Theoretical ending age of primary or basic school education" as specified in Table 1 for Special Educational Needs Programmes in Special Schools.

SECONDARY EDUCATION is from "Theoretical ending age of primary or basic school education" to "Theoretical ending age of generally required school education" as specified in Table 1 for Special Educational Needs Programmes in Special Schools.

ALL YEARS OF COMPULSORY SCHOOLING are from "Theoretical starting age of primary or basic school education" to "Theoretical ending age of generally required school education" as specified in Table 1 for Special Educational Needs Programmes in Special Schools. It is restricted to these years as pilot work established the relative inadequacy of data on special educational needs at pre-primary and post-compulsory stages.

CROSS-NATIONAL CATEGORY A refers to the answer given to Q6. You should consider here those national categories **falling within the resources definition** which were judged to come under cross-national category A (any national categories not falling within the resources definition will not have additional resourcing).

CROSS-NATIONAL CATEGORY B refers to the answer given to Q6. You should consider here those national categories **falling within the resources definition** which were judged to come under cross-national category B (any national categories not falling within the resources definition will not have additional resourcing).

CROSS-NATIONAL CATEGORY C refers to the answer given to Q6. You should consider here those national categories **falling within the resources definition** which were judged to come under cross-national category C (any national categories not falling within the resources definition will not have additional resourcing).

CROSS-NATIONAL CATEGORIES A, B and C refers to all national categories **falling within the resources definition** which were judged to come under the three cross-national categories

TEACHERS refers to persons whose professional activity involves the transmission of knowledge, attitudes and skills as stipulated to students in a specified educational programme (see full definition under notes for Table 2). Relative resources for teachers can be indexed by the relative teacher student ratios of programmes for students with special educational needs in special schools and special classes, and programmes of regular education.

For example, if the relevant ratios are 1 to 30 (regular) and 1 to 8 (special educational needs), the proportional additional resources is 3.75 (*i.e.* 30 divided by 8).

In regular classrooms the computation of relative resources will depend on the formula used.

- For example, a programme for a particular category of special educational need might be given a relative weighting of three compared to the regular programme, such that if a regular class size averages 30, a class with one student following the special educational needs programme is reduced to 28 (*i.e.* 27 + 1x3); with 2 such students to 26 (*i.e.* 24 + 2x3). In this example the relative resource is 3. Such formulae may be based on direct identification of individuals following special educational needs programmes, or on assumptions about the incidence of particular categories of special educational need in integrated settings. In the absence of explicit weighting formulae estimates of the relative teaching resource called for by special educational needs and regular programmes may be feasible.

PROFESSIONAL refers to pedagogical, administrative and professional personnel supporting teachers and students. It includes psychologists, counsellors, speech therapists, physiotherapists and other specialists whose services are particularly important in the special educational needs field. The attempt should be made to assess the relative per capita resourcing across these types of personnel for students in special educational needs and regular programmes.

INDIRECT SUPPORT refers to personnel providing support in areas such as secretarial, clerical, building operations and maintenance, personal services, transport and catering. While several such types of personnel may not differ in proportion in relation to special educational needs and regular programmes others may show substantial differences.

- For example, if special schools in a national system are predominantly residential higher personal services, catering and building related resources will be likely. Similarly, non-residential special schools or classes with wide catchment areas will call for increased transport-related resourcing.

Note that, for the three categories of personnel considered above, the index of relative resourcing is provided by an assessment of the full-time equivalent number of personnel per student for programmes for students with special educational needs relative to typical regular educational programmes.

OECD 2000

FINANCIAL refers to ALL aspects of the resources made available in connection with programmes for students with special educational needs expressed in financial terms.

Hence it includes the three types of personnel resources (**teachers, professional and indirect support**) expressed in relative financial terms. It also includes the financial cost of **Material** resources as defined below and **any other types of resource** made available to support educational programmes for special educational needs.

For example additional teacher training programmes to provide specialist expertise and support curriculum development. In this context, relative resources refers to the total set of resources for programmes for students with special educational needs relative to that for a typical regular programme, per capita, with each expressed in financial terms

MATERIAL refers to "non-human" resources such as hearing and sight aids, mechanical aids, mobility aids and any other resources which help those with special educational needs to access the curriculum. As, typically, such material resources are only made available to those with special educational needs it is not feasible to develop an index of relative resources for this aspect considered in isolation.

Notes: **Multiple categorisation and resourcing.** In general the study has not attempted to grapple with the issues involved in students being multiply categorised (*i.e.* being considered to fall under two or more categories of special educational need) – however see section on multiple categorisation above. It is understood that some countries operate systems where students considered to fall under two or more categories receive further resourcing (*e.g.* following a multiplicative or additive rule). Please annotate for this giving the rule followed.

Additional resource information. It is appreciated that the amount of information available on the resourcing of special educational needs varies widely from country to country. If further information on resourcing is readily available it would be appreciated if this were to be included with the response to this instrument.

ANNOTATION SHEET   NUMBER OF SHEET: _____ OF _____

Table/Row/Column	Annotation

OECD PUBLICATIONS, 2, rue André-Pascal, 75775 PARIS CEDEX 16
PRINTED IN FRANCE
(96 2000 06 1 P 1) ISBN 92-64-17689-6 – No. 51301 2000